D1095776

ACHIEVEMENT IN AMERICAN POETRY

LOUISE BOGAN

ACHIEVEMENT IN
AMERICAN POETRY

 GATEWAY EDITIONS, INC.

Distributed by HENRY REGNERY COMPANY

LOS ANGELES   CHICAGO   NEW YORK

ACKNOWLEDGMENTS

For permission to reprint we wish to make acknowledgment:

To Appleton-Century-Crofts, Inc. for "The Flower-Fed Buffaloes" from *Going to the Stars* by Vachel Lindsay, copyright 1926 by D. Appleton & Company. To Brandt and Brandt for "Cherish You Then the Hope I Shall Forget" from *Second April* by Edna St. Vincent Millay, published by Harper and Brothers, copyright 1920 and 1948 by Edna St. Vincent Millay; for "Truce for a Moment" from *Huntsman, What Quarry?* by Edna St. Vincent Millay, published by Harper and Brothers, copyright 1933, 1934, 1936, 1937, 1938, and 1939 by Edna St. Vincent Millay. To Harcourt, Brace and Company, Inc. for "Mélange adultère de tout" and for "Marina" from *Collected Poems of T. S. Eliot;* for "Christmas Eve by Hooker's Statue" from *Lord Weary's Castle* by Robert Lowell; for "In the Elegy Season" from *Ceremony and Other Poems* by Richard Wilbur; for "Troop Train" from *V-Letter and Other Poems* by Karl Shapiro. To Henry Holt and Company, Inc. for "Band Concert" from *Cornhuskers* by Carl Sandburg, copyright 1946 by Carl Sandburg; for "The Pasture" and "After Apple-picking" from *Complete Poems of Robert Frost,* copyright 1930, 1949 by Henry Holt and Company, Inc.

To Houghton Mifflin Company for "Cirque d'hiver" by Elizabeth Bishop from *North and South,* 1946; for "In the Reading-Room of the British Museum" from *A Roadside Harp* by Louise Imogen Guiney, 1893. To Alfred A. Knopf, Inc. for "The Black Riders" and "Places Among the Stars" from *Collected Poems of Stephen Crane,* copyright 1922 by William H. Crane; for "Bronze Trumpets and Sea Water" from *Collected Poems of Elinor Wylie,* copyright 1921, 1932 by Alfred A. Knopf, Inc.; for "Felo de Se" from *Collected Poems of Elinor Wylie,* copyright 1929, 1932 by Alfred A. Knopf, Inc.; for "The Emperor of Ice Cream" and "To the Roaring Wind" from *Harmonium* by Wallace Stevens, copyright 1923, 1931 by Alfred A. Knopf, Inc.; for "Piazza Piece" from *Selected Poems* by John Crowe Ransom, copyright 1927, 1945 by Alfred A. Knopf, Inc. To Little, Brown and Company for "The Soul Selects Her Own Society," "Hope Is the Thing with Feathers," and "Except the Smaller Size" from *Poems by Emily Dickinson,* ed. by Martha D. Bianchi and A. L. Hampson, copyright 1914, 1942 by Martha Dickinson Bianchi. To Liveright Publishing Corporation for "Air Plant" and "Hurricane" from *The Collected Poems of Hart Crane* published by Liveright Publishing Corp., copyright by Liveright, Inc., 1933; for "Orchard" from *Collected Poems of H. D.* [Hilda Doolittle], published by Liveright Publishing Corp., copyright by Boni & Liveright, Inc., 1925.

To The Macmillan Company for "I Shall Not Care" from *Rivers to the Sea* by Sara Teasdale, copyright 1915 by The Macmillan Company; for "The Paper Nautilus" from *What Are Years* by Marianne Moore, copyright 1914 by The Macmillan Company; for "Bewick Finzer" and "New England" from *Collected Poems* by Edwin Arlington Robinson, copyright 1934 by The Macmillan Company. To New Directions for "Come My Cantilations" from *Poems from Blast,* for "Liu Ch'e" from *Lustra,* and for "E. P. Ode pour L'Election de Son Sepulchre" from *Hugh Selwyn Mauberly; Life and Contacts* by Ezra Pound, copyright 1926 by Ezra Pound; for selections I and XXI from *Spring and All,*

I-XXVIII by William Carlos Williams, copyright 1938 by New Directions. To Random House, Inc. for "Cattivo Tempo" and "For T. S. Eliot and His Sixtieth Birthday" from *Nones* by W. H. Auden, copyright 1951 by W. H. Auden. To Rinehart & Co., Inc., for "In Time of Grief" from *The Selected Poems of Lizette Woodworth Reese,* copyright 1926 by Rinehart & Co., Inc., and for "Inscription for a Library," from *A Victorian Village* by Lizette Woodworth Reese, copyright 1929 by Rinehart & Co., Inc. To Charles Scribner's Sons for "Mr. Pope," reprinted from *Poems* 1922-1947 by Allen Tate, copyright 1928, 1948 by Charles Scribner's Sons; for "Of Course Not," reprinted from *Strike Through the Mask!* by Peter Viereck, copyright 1950 by Peter Viereck. To William Sloane Associates, Inc. for "Country Summer" from *High Falcon* by Léonie Adams, copyright 1929 by Léonie Adams. And to Ellen C. Masters for "Petit the Poet" from the *Spoon River Anthology* by Edgar Lee Masters. Also to Random House, Inc., for permission to use "Water Raining" and "Food: Custard," from *Tender Buttons* by Gertrude Stein.

Our thanks are also due Henry A. Stickney, brother of the poet, for his gracious permission to use "Mnemosyne" from *The Poems of Trumbull Stickney*.

CONTENTS

ACHIEVEMENT IN AMERICAN POETRY

I

AMERICAN POETRY IN 1900: BACKGROUND AND AUDIENCE

FORMAL POETRY in America in the year 1900 seemed benighted in every sense: it was imitative, sentimental, and "genteel." Its relationship to the vigorous elements in the culture which surrounded it—and there were many—was superficial. Its relationship to the vigorous poetic talents which only recently had ceased functioning was weak; both Whitman and Melville, in the preceding decade, had died in obscurity, and the brief flurry of interest in the poems and letters of Emily Dickinson, beginning in 1890, had already died out.

The weight of British Victorian tradition lay heavily upon American poets in general; and the strong native moralizing bent of the American poets of the school readers—Bryant, Whittier, and Longfellow—still operated. A feeble reflection from the English aesthetic movement of the eighties and nineties was also apparent, but recently this influence had been stigmatized morally and more or less forced underground, both in England and America, by the scandal attendant upon the trial and conviction, in 1896, of Oscar Wilde.

The general culture in the United States, at the beginning of the twentieth century, was itself awkward and provisional. It was a newly "citified" and suburbanized culture: "a life by imitation," in the words of Frank Lloyd Wright, "spread wide and thin over the vast surface of a continent." A new spirit of showiness and frivolity was beginning to modify a basically rural and fundamentalist point of view;

the ideals of "the gilded age" of the seventies and eighties were spreading over larger areas and infiltrating into all levels of the population. That a vital gaiety and remnants of pioneer vigor existed, beneath the general gimcrack atmosphere of the times, is proved by the public's fondness for music, and for forms of entertainment which had not yet become either wholly commercialized or mechanized. Many connections with true folk tradition had been lost, but there was an audience for ragtime and the brass band, for musical comedy and operetta, for vaudeville and the circus.[1]

The energy of folk poetry was, however, at this time and for years to come, rigidly separated from the formal poetry of the period by barriers of taste. The one exception to this rule was the negro spiritual, which Stedman had recognized by including examples in his *American Anthology* (1900) and which had been mentioned by Thomas Wentworth Higginson in *The Atlantic Monthly* back in the late sixties. A fresh breath of primitive life had been injected into American prose by Mark Twain and others, and the nineties had shown a marked interest in dialect prose and poetry—folk at second hand—but the "serious" verse flowed insipidly on, quite undisturbed by these popular eddies. American prose was already far closer to the true sources of creativeness than American poetry showed any signs of being. William Dean Howells in his later phase, Hamlin Garland, and others were already alive to the mingled streams of American life and to the turmoil beneath its surface—to civic corruption, to social injustice, and to the dog-eat-dog morality of a time of ruthless industrial expansion.

---

1. A semicritical "popular" humor showed up in Finley Peter Dunne's "Mr. Dooley," George Ade's *Fables in Slang,* and in the newspaper cartoons of John T. McCutcheon and others.

The chief arbiters of the literary world of the time, almost without exception, were men whose timidity of spirit matched the shallowness of their experience of life. Mark Twain had sunk into the bitter cynicism of his old age; the New England intellectual tradition (in which, as early as 1843, Emerson had detected signs of "hollow dilettantism") had proved stronger, even in its decline, than Western energy. Smallness of vision and conventionality of outlook were now being infected with an active fear and dislike of any true creative innovations; these were held to be either vulgar or bizarre. And the active, though hidden, force of moral criteria, in the form of active censorship and "comstockery," was soon to become more and more apparent, as originality began to force itself through.

It should be stated at the outset that the judging of the merit of a work of art by a set of moralistic and materialist values was by no means a purely American habit. This system of valuation had become important in Europe at large, and most especially in England, since the early nineteenth century. Not only a new public, but a new set of "publics" was brought into being by the profound and far-reaching social and economic changes which followed upon the end of the Napoleonic Wars. The existence of various levels of appreciation, as well as various levels of excellence, in the arts as a whole, was a fact which did not appeal to middle-class thinking; and it was a bourgeois "ruling taste" which soon became everywhere entrenched and powerful. In England, after Coleridge (who understood the situation at its beginning) few voices were raised against "ideals" of respectability applied to art and to literature. In France, on the other hand, novelists and poets, from Stendhal and Balzac, Baudelaire and

Flaubert, immediately began to analyze the oppressive situation in which they found themselves with the utmost vigor and clear-sightedness. The constant shifts of political influence no doubt helped to keep alive this power, in certain French writers, to separate the creative from the false, as the nineteenth century advanced; this unbroken French tradition of active criticism was to become, as we shall see, a decisive factor in the final break-through of a modern aesthetic, in all artistic fields, in the twentieth century.

Two basic cravings, on the part of the bourgeois population, were for comfort and for entertainment; reading matter in new forms catered to both. Literature soon became a kind of commodity, produced and promoted according to commercial means; Sainte-Beuve early comments on this phenomenon. Coleridge realized the insatiable desire for amusement in the English reading public of his day. He makes (*circa* 1820) a typical citizen express a typical view:

"It may be all very deep and clever; but really one ought to be quite sure of it before one wrenches one's brain to find out what it is. I take up a Book as a Companion, with whom I can have an easy cheerful chit-chat on what we both know beforehand, or else on matters of fact. In our leisure hours we have a right to relaxation and amusement."

And Coleridge, in the same series of notes, goes on to give an analysis of the changes in literary emphasis and direction that had moulded the citizen's opinion:

In former times a *popular* work meant one that adapted the *results* of a studious meditation or scientific research to the capacity of the people, presenting in the concrete, by instances and examples, what has been ascertained in the abstract and by discovery of the Law. *Now*, on the other hand, that is a popular work which gives back to the people their own errors and prejudices, and flatters the many by creating them, under the title of *The Public*, into a supreme and unappellate *Tribunal of Intellectual Excellence*.

For some time it has been clear how thoroughly, and with what tragic results, certain English Victorian poets and artists of great original endowment were drawn from their proper function, into the place and function assigned to them by popular demands. Few poets of the nineteenth century withstood these demands; Tennyson is the chief unhappy example of those who did not. It is, therefore, not surprising that many American poets, surrounded by a comparatively young and still colonial-minded culture, should have succumbed to like pressures.

ii

It is evident that British and American poetry shared a common need as the twentieth century began: the need to discover a way through to emotional, intellectual, and factual truth—to a truth undisturbed either by dogmatic opinion, distorting prejudice, or shifting fashion. Fresh sources of moral, as well as of aesthetic, courage had to be opened up, in order that the brutalizing effects of materialism, and the narrowness of provincial thinking and feeling, could be combated. The forces of the imagination had to be renewed and human values had to be restated in imaginative terms.

The barriers to this renewal of force were so long established, in English-speaking countries, that it was apparent, even at the time, that some linkage would have to be forged between a thoroughly Victorianized England, between an America in which many Victorian moral derivatives existed and some foreign fields wherein purer aesthetic motives and cruder creative strength had been allowed, for one reason

or another, to develop in comparative freedom. As it
turned out, these fields were Ireland and France.

The story of the Irish literary renaissance cannot
be outlined here—although Yeats' career, in its later
phase, constitutes a direct influence in American
poetry after 1912. It is important, however, to describe briefly the aesthetic development in France,
since that development, once described, can be held
as a constant point of reference; and since this full,
lively, and continually growing modern aesthetic
movement was to influence and intersect American
poetic achievement at many important points. In
fact, large areas of French artistic knowledge and
practice were to be absorbed by Americans in an
extremely short space of time.

Because middle-class ruling taste never succeeded
in making a thorough conquest of French artists and
thinkers, it is possible to trace in France with clarity
and directness the forces which have always moulded
aesthetic sensibility. Two sets of pressures exist. The
first is the pressures applied to the arts from their
exterior environment: social, political and philosophic. The second is a more subtle complex of
forces which operate within the art itself: impulses
toward vitality and vision which keep any art constantly open to renewal.

The atmosphere of French art as the nineteenth
century ended, was one of impressionism. The history of the impressionist movement in general is long
and involved. Several points concerning it, however,
can be easily recognized. It was a movement which
had an initial impulse in the fact that the nineteenth-
century French painter found himself free from
allegiances to institutions of church or state. If he
did not succumb to popular demands he had no public; he could paint as he pleased. At the same period,

developments within art itself were about to free him from any further interest in direct representation. "For almost five hundred years," writes Sir Kenneth Clark, "artists had been applying their skill to an imitation of nature. During this time numerous methods of representation had been mastered, culminating with a method (impressionism) which resolved light by a new combination of science and subtlety of vision. By 1900 the more adventurous and original artists had lost interest in painting facts. By a common and powerful impulse they were driven to abandon the imitation of natural appearances."[2] Anecdote and "reality" were left to the newly invented camera.

The development of impressionism in painting was accompanied by developments with similar aims, in music and in literature. In French music, with Debussy and his followers, logical harmonic progression began to be abandoned in favor of subtleties of modulation hitherto unexplored; in both France and Germany the strictness of the sonata form was being dissolved into the freedom of the tone poem. In poetry the same turn toward purity, "innerness," and delicacy of nuance can be recognized in the work of the symbolist school, the poems of whose leader, Mallarmé, stood at the junction of poetry and music. With Mallarmé poetry began to turn away from "meaning" as painting had turned away from "representation"; and as the early symbolist poets had drawn inspiration from Wagner's operas, so now musicians began to base their works upon poetry. Debussy's *L'Après-midi d'une faune* and his symbolist opera *Pelléas et Mélisande,* both strongly literary in derivation, were composed in 1902.

---

2. See Clark's *Landscape Painting.*

These European tendencies to dissolve form in the arts, and at the same time to merge one art with another, herald the beginning of an interest in subconscious and irrational processes which was to become more and more evident as the twentieth century advanced in time. The researches of Edouard von Hartmann, the writings of Nietzsche, the mysticism of Strindberg and Ibsen had already made themselves felt in European thought. The perfect and unbroken image of Renaissance man was being broken into segments; the heavy weight of materialist and positivist thought was being alleviated; a new, and a tragic, human frailty was being discovered piecemeal—along with new and mysterious sources of human strength. A shift of emphasis was about to take place, from the physical world to the world of the spirit, or of the psyche, to use a purely secular term. The time was already at hand when scientific findings would reinforce artistic intuition; when philosophy, with Bergson, would explore time in terms of memory; when a rigid mechanical universe, based on law, would be transformed into a fluid one, based on inferences.

The history of American poetry in the last fifty years is in part the history of a connection made between these European sources of living thought and feeling. The connection was not easily accomplished, as will be seen; the way of its accomplishment was made rough by resentment and ridicule. Native American sources of power had to be opened and made available by means which, at first glance, seem quite inapplicable, if not actually coarse and vulgar. The history of the American arts from 1900 on is often a record of successful flank attacks made by "outsiders" upon an entrenchment of taste and techniques against which straightforward frontal attacks would have failed.

II

THE FORERUNNERS: NEWSPAPERMEN AND BOHEMIANS

THE NEWSPAPER, in America, had been the training school for many writers. Young backwoodsmen like Mark Twain had learned to set type as youths, and later, as reporters, went out to gather news and meet "life" at first hand. Both Poe and Whitman, in cities of the Eastern seaboard, had worked for newspapers; and many young Southern writers had the same background of journalist experience. By 1900, American journalism was well into its more sensational, or "yellow" stage; and young Alfred Harmsworth had made researches into American methods before founding, in England, the halfpenny *Daily Mail* (1896) "for busy men," and following it by *The Daily Mirror* (1903). The tactics of this new journalism were far more ruthless than those of the old; they were designed to influence the reader's opinion by emotional means; and their power was felt in both the Boer and the Cuban wars.

To the American man of letters, the newspaperman, even in his new and romantic role of "special correspondent," was a writer who functioned on a distinctly low and vulgar level. Yet it was from this level that strong oblique blows were about to be struck, which were to shatter conventional literary citadels from foundations to summit. One of the first of these blows came from a Midwestern novelist who had worked on newspapers in Chicago, in the old Mississippi River cities, in Pittsburgh, and finally in New York. This young writer was Theodore Dreiser, whose first novel *Sister Carrie* told American truths

as they had never been told before. *Sister Carrie,*
first published in 1900, was almost immediately suppressed by its own publisher.

Newspapermen, along with theatrical people, furnished a professional core to those locales that had
come into being as the cities grew: the urban
"Bohemias." In America, these Bohemias differed
from their European counterparts in having more
frontier color and energy. They had appeared at an
early period in the prerailroad cities along the great
river routes from New Orleans to Cincinnati and St.
Louis; and very early in San Francisco, where frontier riches brought in popular sophistication. These
cities often had their own newspapers and opera
houses; they were visited by traveling road com-
panies; their population was shifting and diversified;
they were often the centers of a moral freedom strikingly in contrast to the rural puritanisms of the country at large. Westward emigration, after the Civil
War, added foreign influence—German, Polish, and
Czech—and negro music began to drift northward
into Missouri and Illinois. These urban centers of
comparative freedom and gaiety (which often coincided almost exactly with urban underworlds) attracted writers, artists, and musicians—and outcasts,
misfits, and amateurs of various degrees of talent and
peculiarity as well. The new and powerful talents in
many fields were almost without exception to be influenced by their contact with these areas, on the
fringe of respectable America, from the nineties on-
ward. For America's Bohemias at that time were
authentic. They held the seeds of an evolving American reality: the rebellion of an intelligent and gifted
minority against the platitudes and insipidities of a
growing "business" culture. Here dissenters could

express themselves—against village parochialism, social injustice, and brainless shows of wealth and power.

Several levels of Bohemia existed: all were more open and gay than the life that surrounded them. On the lower level—in beer gardens, shabby saloons, cheap cafés and in shabby lodgings—a kind of urban hedge-schoolmastering went on: an exchange of ideas, enthusiasms, scattered and fragmentary experiences of European arts and ways of life, between young and old, foreigner and native. On the higher level more prosperous men and women circulated from restaurant to restaurant, in a gaslit night life; from theater to music hall, from concert hall to opera and picture gallery, continually appraising America in European terms and, more often than not, spreading the news of current European art and literature. The most tireless of these enthusiasts were often amateurs of at least one art and were frequently journalists. The most brilliant example of this type was James Gibbon Huneker (1860-1921).

ii

Huneker was not a complete amateur in the arts; he began his career as a professional pianist and teacher. Born in Philadelphia and at first drawn to the law, he early made the piano his chief interest and studied at the Paris Conservatory and later with Rafael Joseffy. As Joseffy's assistant, he taught piano in New York for ten years. He began his journalist career in 1887 with a column of comment and gossip in the monthly, *The Musical Observer*. His interests widened, and he began to include dramatists, painters, philosophers—principally Nietzsche —in his brilliant discussions which, after 1891, appeared in the *New York Evening Record* and other New York newspapers as daily features. Later he

was widely syndicated. "The vivacity and penetra-
tion of [Huneker's] comments attracted immediate
and wide attention," one biographer writes; and
H. L. Mencken, who learned much from Huneker in
his own apprentice years, speaks of the tremendous
contrast between Huneker's varied interests and
"cosmopolitan" point of view, and those of the
typical professional critic of the time, who, in contrast, seemed "no more than a talented sophomore
or, at best, a somewhat absurd professor." "Huneker," Mencken adds, "was the one critical performer
who could rouse his audience to anything approaching enthusiasm. [Moreover] nine times out of ten,
in estimating a new man in music or letters, he came
curiously close to the truth at the first attempt . . .
and always announced his opinion in good time: his
solo has always preceded the chorus."

Huneker had, in his highly original manner, expressed his views of Nietzsche in 1888; of Shaw the
critic in the years 1886-1900; and later, of Ibsen and
Strindberg and French impressionist painting. He
early recognized the importance of the first American
realists in the field of the novel: Stephen Crane
(whom he knew), Frank Norris, Dreiser, and H. B.
Fuller; and he praised the American realist painters
Luks, Sloan, and Prendergast soon after their appearance in 1908. Throughout the first decades of
the century he continued to bring into sight and into
focus, for American readers, all he had seen, heard,
and read at home and abroad. Mencken characteristically sums up Huneker's achievement in the Introduction he wrote for Huneker's *Essays* (1920):

He cleared the grove . . . of the shrill fugelmen of bad
painting, maudlin music, valentine poetry, tin-pot drama and
bogus criticism. He brought in a clearer air. . . . The art
of criticism, as [his contemporaries] practised it, was a
branch of Christian endeavor. Huneker related it to living

ideas, to all the great movement of human forces, to life itself. The world to him was a single entity, and each of the
arts was a brother to the other. No man could have been
less a reformer by inclination and yet he became a reformer
beyond compare. He emancipated American criticism from
its old bondage to sentimentality and stupidity, and with it
he emancipated all the arts themselves.

Huneker's direct heirs included Mencken, Paul
Rosenfeld, and others. The Huneker method of approach may seem showy and shallow to a later generation who demand that criticism bear heavier
weights of meaning and utilize sharper tools of analysis; but there is no doubt that Huneker broke up the
critical tameness and rigidity of his time in the most
effective manner by which they could then be as-
saulted—by sheer idiosyncratic taste expressed with
point and color. And the fact that he functioned for
many years in a field where his energy and insight
could make a direct impact on a large audience—in
the field of daily journalism—seems, in retrospect,
providential in the extreme.

iii

The recruiting of literary talents by newspapers to
serve as special correspondents was new in the nineties; and the figure of Stephen Crane, correspondent
in two wars, must stand at the beginning (although
in a rather unformulated relation) of any discussion
of modern American poetry. Crane's two books of
free verse, *Black Riders* (1895) and *War Is Kind*
(1899), published in his twenty-fourth and twenty-
eighth years, brought into American poetry, naïvely
and almost by chance, certain effects which French
poets had already worked out at length and in detail;
and foreshadowed imagist effects that were to come.
Crane's brief writing career had blazed into sensational prominence with the publication of *The Red*

Badge of Courage in 1895. Born in 1871 in Newark,
New Jersey, Crane had worked on newspapers since
boyhood. He evolved for himself a style—staccato,
tense, and bare—which he later called "impressionist." "Impressionism was his faith," a friend has
recorded. "Impressionism was truth, and no man
could be great who was not an impressionist. For
greatness consisted in knowing the truth." Wherever
Crane had come upon this term, upon which he
based so much conviction—and he may have found
it in the accounts of the Ruskin-Whistler trial—it is
interesting to find the word on the lips of an American writer at that particular period.

Crane's talent—natural and instinctive—was of a
true impressionist kind. It developed hardly at all;
Crane carried his initial awkwardness, as well as his
early brilliance, practically unchanged throughout his
short career. His lines of verse are slightly warped
by an affectation he inherited from his time, as well
as by an adolescent irony he was unable either to
develop or conceal. The poems came to him spon-
taneously; his head was full of them, and he could
write them down in any favorable surroundings.
This spontaneity gives them their value. They are
less literary productions than moments of resolved
conflict, and as such they point toward, and expose,
sources of poetic power long unexplored in American
poetic practice.

Crane (1871-1900) is linked to Emily Dickinson
(1830-1886), whose posthumous volume, *Poems,*
edited by her friends, Thomas Wentworth Higginson
and Mabel Todd Lewis, was published in 1890. This
small volume, with the poet's favorite Indian pipe
stamped in gold upon its cover, had made an im-
pression upon the literary arbiters of the decade;
William Dean Howells had read certain Dickinson

poems to Crane, before Crane wrote *Black Riders*. Thus two disparate and unlike American creative lives intersected. Emily Dickinson, seemingly a New England spinster of the classic type and sharing many of the type's oddities of character, was dead at fifty-six. She was, except among her family and friends, quite without fame or honor. On the other hand, Stephen Crane, the young journalist caught up into the turmoil of his time, participated in metropolitan squalor and glitter. He looked for local color in Mexico and the Far West, was an amateur gold-runner between Florida and Cuba, a war correspondent in Cuba and Greece, a Bohemian and finally an expatriate in the England of Henry James, Joseph Conrad and the other writers at the forefront of new literary times and new literary manners. And Crane was dead at twenty-eight in the midst of his fame.

III

THE LINE OF TRUTH AND THE LINE
OF FEELING

A SECOND SITUATION, directly in contrast to gregarious Bohemian life, proved to be favorable to the development of American poetic talent at the turn of the century. This was the situation of the poet in almost complete isolation, separated by some special set of conditions from American society. The story of the gifted person, cut off in one way or another from full participation in the life of his day, was not a new one in America. At best, that isolation gave such a person perspective; at worst, it turned him into an eccentric.

Edwin Arlington Robinson, born in 1869 in the village of Head Tide, Maine, spent his youth and young manhood in the neighboring town of Gardiner. He entered Harvard in 1891 and spent two years there as a special student. From 1893 to 1897 he was forced—by poverty and a tragic family situation—to live in Gardiner, completely cut off, except for one or two friends, from any direct contacts with literature or with a normal social life. He was forced to turn his attention to the characters of his neighbors, many similarly trapped and some even more hopelessly. His own nature was sensitive without being rich; he inherited the laconic speech and the dry sense of humor of the New England townsman; and his bent was toward realism. He was attracted by the work of Zola and by the "simple accuracy" of Crabbe, and wrote sonnets to both. Kipling, incongruously enough, was another influence. Through a long series of trials and errors (he attempted, for a time, to write in prose) he finally evolved a poetic style and point of view. He published, at his own expense, a small volume, *The Torrent and the Night Before,* in 1896; and in the following year what must stand as Robinson's first book (in which a good deal of the former small volume was reprinted), *The Children of the Night,* appeared.

The Children of the Night is one of the hinges upon which American poetry was able to turn from the sentimentality of the nineties toward modern veracity and psychological truth. It is filled with portraits of men who are misfits when they are not actual outcasts; and into each is incorporated something of Robinson's own lonely and eccentric nature. The secret dreamer, the lonely old roisterer, the enigmatic dandy, the baffled lover, the cynic and the suicide—all are filled with an acute but ambiguous bitterness, and at the same time are touched in with the utmost delicacy and tenderness of understanding. Robinson, with the sympathy of a brother in misfortune, notes their failures and degradations without losing sight of their peculiar courage. The structure of these early poems is impeccably correct although subtly varied. Their originality lies in their tone, and in their diction. Robinson, from the beginning, was able to twist the clichés of sentimental poetry to a wry originality. His vocabulary and idiom were based squarely on the everyday New England speech of his period; and his rhythms are often exactly the rhythm of that speech. To reproduce these rhythms was in itself a triumph at the time. The native witticisms, which appear so delightfully in "Mr. Flood's Party" were themselves formal and fixed; Robinson knew this and treated them with a fitting poetic formality. Robinson never completely lost this peculiar coloring; the dry native strand is woven into even the most nebulous and complicated work of his later period. And if his beliefs, based on a Protestant small-town skepticism, never greatly enlarged, neither did they wear down into insignificance through the abrasion of time and subsequent experience.

He went to New York in 1897, and this move took him straight into the shabbiest level of the urban Bohemia. His subsequent career, for the many years in which he endured poverty, was shadowed and disturbed by a series of nightmarish events. An almost defenseless man, of the utmost delicacy and sensibility, he—like many of his kind—seemed to attract his grotesque opposites. His lack of defenses and his weaknesses laid him open—not only to the habit of drink, but to the threat of blackmail from scoundrelly companions; he was forced by poverty to endure the role of "the poet in the subway," before Theodore Roosevelt, then President, found him a routine position in the customs service. His subsequent release from a life of fantastic hardship, through the efforts of his friends and the kindly aid of Mrs. MacDowell, gave him the leisure to write his later works. The story of his ultimate literary success belongs to a later decade.

Robinson's reaction to events and his conclusions concerning human life and destiny continued to be based on the idealism of his youth, to which was added a simple variety of agnosticism and stoicism. His later long poems, in which he adumbrated rather than described a set of human actions, are, it is evident, profoundly symbolic. Robinson's symbols in these poems have never been thoroughly analyzed; but there is no doubt that they hold the key to the ambiguities of his nature. They were his obsessions rather than his creations, and they were repetitive obsessions as time went on. His tenuosities of lan-

guage served to disguise them, so that the poet could
bring them up to consciousness; they are never figures of human life, but of fear, bafflement, ambival-
ence, and despair.

It is important, finally, to recognize in Robinson
an end product of a New England town civilization.
He has no affiliation with what New England towns-
people term "the countryman." He is allied, in this
respect, to Emerson, Thoreau, and Emily Dickinson—all natives of New England towns as opposed
to the actual New England country dweller, whose
character and viewpoint Robert Frost was later not
only to describe in his work, but to exemplify, in
part, in his life and person.

ii

It is clear that Robinson, in spite of his central
contribution to poetic truth, did little to reconstitute
any revivifying warmth of feeling in the poetry of his
time. This task, it is now evident, was accomplished
almost entirely by women poets through methods
which proved to be as strong as they seemed to be
delicate. The whole involved question of woman as
artist cannot be dealt with here. We can at this point
only follow the facts, as they unfold from the later
years of the nineteenth century to the beginning of
the twentieth; these facts prove that the line of poetic
intensity which wavers and fades out and often completely fails in poetry written by men, on the feminine side moves on unbroken. Women, as "intuitive" beings, are less open to the success and failures,
the doubts and despair which attack reason's mech-
anisms. Women's feeling, at best, is closely attached
to the organic heart of life, and their psychic processes operate according to rules which have never
been fully discovered or explored. These womanly

attributes have been always acknowledged, if not fully in the world of reality, at least widely in the world of myth.

Women, it is true, contributed in a large measure to the general leveling, dilution, and sentimentalization of verse, as well as of prose, during the nineteenth century. Their successes in the field of the sentimental novel had been overpowering; and their "poetic" ambitions were boundless. The American literary tradition, from the time of seventeenth-century Ann Bradstreet ("The Tenth Muse Lately Sprung up in America") had never been without an outstanding American woman "singer." Mrs. Sigourney had occupied this role over a protracted period—her life extended from the year of Washington's second Presidency to that of Lincoln's death—and she had successors. Women's verse of this popular variety reflected with deadly accuracy every change in the nation's sentimental tendencies. Rufus Griswold's *Female Poets of America,* at its first appearance in 1849, is filled with grim thoughts of death, along with a compensating piety and sanctimoniousness. A later version of this work, published in the seventies under another editor, shows a marked change both in tone and subject matter. Women versifiers after the Civil War were more airy and more ardent; and the treatment of subjects formerly forbidden—wine drinking, theatergoing, and the like—became usual. These women of the "gilded age" also began to show a strong interest in "culture;" the volume is scattered through with verses "inspired" by this or that work of art.

The most striking change in women's verse at this time was its new treatment of the subject of love between the sexes. It was Ella Wheeler (later Mrs. Ella Wheeler Wilcox), a young and vocal girl from a Wisconsin farm, who brought into popular love poetry the element of "sin." She published *Poems of Passion* in 1886. By 1900 a whole feminine school of rather daring verse on the subject of feminine and masculine emotions had followed Mrs. Wilcox's lead. In this thoroughly middle-class "poetic" *genre,* the combination of an air of the utmost respectability with the wildest sort of implications was strange indeed. The great number of women who had taken to rhythm and meter as a form of self-expression can be traced in Stedman's *An American Anthology* (1900), where the list of women with three (and sometimes four) respectable Yankee names moves steadily down the page of contents.

It is all the more remarkable, in view of this redoubtable and often completely ridiculous record of sentimental feminine attitudinizing in verse, that true, compelling, and sincere women's talents were able to emerge. Sentimental poetry on the middle level was never destroyed—it operates in full and unimpeded force at the present day; but an authentic current began to run beside it. The first signs of feminine song from a true source were so fragile that they were easily overlooked. The obscure publication in 1887 of Lizette Woodworth Reese's *A Branch of May* announced the new feminine sincerity of emotion and approach. Miss Reese, a native of Baltimore and a school teacher throughout her life, wrote her lyrics well outside the conventional literary scene, in what were then rural and provincial surroundings. She conveyed her emotions by means of an almost weightless diction and by a syntax so natural that its art was very nearly imperceptible. The romantic locutions and faded ornaments of the nineteenth-century lyric here drop away; expression is molded by feeling as the liquid in a glass is shaped by the glass itself. Even the slightest affectation becomes evident, as basic emotional simplicity begins to find basic technical simplicity. Miss Reese might be a young woman talking to herself in a garden, but this colloquy with the self is accomplished in form. Her pure and delicately repetitive gift remained unchanged throughout her long lifetime (she died in 1935); her later works showed only a further distillation and concentration of form and material.

Louise Imogen Guiney (1861-1920), a Catholic New Englander with a wider range of interest and a more dramatic style than Miss Reese, had published *Songs at the Start* in 1884. Miss Guiney's interest in the English Carolinian and Recusant poets of the seventeenth century gave her work a learned base; she wrote in a gallant spirit which foreshadowed the more masculine attitudes of certain women poets of the twenties. Her lyrics, however, are frequently as exquisite and as seemingly effortless as those of her Maryland contemporary.

And it is at this point that we must deal with the first appearance in print of Emily Dickinson (1830-1886). Her first volume, *Poems,* was published posthumously, in 1890 (with, it may be added, considerable success; it went through six printings in six weeks). The poems of this volume were arranged, according to the taste of the day, under "moral" headings: Love, Nature, God, and the like; and their eccentricities had been somewhat softened by the editors. The selection was characterized, moreover, by a slight accent on the poet's more arch and pertly "childlike" side; but her more extraordinary qualities were also apparent from the first. The full discovery and appreciation of these qualities belong to the second decade of this century; but that they did not go entirely unrecognized by her close contemporaries is proved by the fact that two volumes of poetry and one of letters appeared after 1890, during a short period of six years.

The first imprint of Emily Dickinson's genius belongs, therefore, to the nineties, along with the first imprint of Robinson's. It is the last imprint in American literature of New England town culture in the pure tradition; although Miss Dickinson's New England strain had advanced straight from Puritan mores, untouched, and even repelled, by Unitarian reform. And while Robinson's form had been influenced by European and British culture, Dickinson's showed no such influence. Behind the Dickinson stanza stands the hymn, and the hymn alone.

Freshness and sincerity of emotion, and economical directness of method were, it can be seen, early apparent in formal poetry written by women well before the turn of the century. Women's subsequent rejection of moral passivity, economic dependence, and intellectual listlessness in favor of active interests and an involvement with the world around them—a rejection which, at crucial moments in the English suffragist movement, became exteriorized in actual physical combat—changed the direction and tone of their writing. This transition was not accomplished without the formation of new compensating tensions, nor without collisions with the basic rules of "respectability." That women were not forced to waste too much of their time and energy in social and spiritual improvisation during this period of transition, is in great measure due to the fact that certain women, early in the situation, had been able to project their emotions through the medium of art; they had advanced into new "freedoms," accompanied by their own works of passion and imagination. If they began their break with some of the naïve gestures of the amateur, they were to conclude it with the full invigorating knowledge of the ways and means of the artist.

IV

THE BREAK-THROUGH BEGINS, 1900-1912

THE FIRST ten years of the twentieth century is of
particular interest in the story of the development of
the American arts. First, it was the period when
realism finally emerged in the novel and in painting.
Second, American inventive genius began to take
positive hold with those machines which were to
change every aspect of American life: the automo-
bile, the moving picture camera and projector, and
the airplane. Third, it was the last period when a
wide cleavage and time lag between American and
European art, ways of thought, and mores in general
was to exist. Lastly, it was the time when the American critical faculty began to apply itself to the facts
of American civilization—from those of civic and
business corruption to those of arts and letters.

Holdovers from an agricultural era showed up
chiefly in moralistic prejudices. These prejudices had
fanatical fringes that constantly impeded any show
of literary daring or originality: Anthony Comstock
was active in the New York Society for the Suppression of Vice, and Boston had its Watch and Ward
Society. Secondary education offered youth the study
and appreciation of Sir Walter Scott's *Marmion*
(1808) and *The Lady of the Lake* (1810), along
with Tennyson's *The Idylls of the King* (1859-72).
And we have direct information as to the level upon
which English literature was taught in the universities
in the evidence of T. S. Eliot.[1]

---

1. In *An Examination of Ezra Pound,* edited by Peter Russell
(New York, New Directions, 1950), p. 25.

Whatever may have been the literary scene in America between the beginning of the century and the year 1914, it remains in my mind a complete blank. . . . Undergraduates at Harvard in my time read the English poets of the '90s who were dead: that was as near as we could get to any living tradition. Certainly I cannot remember any English poet then alive who contributed to my own education. . . . I do not think it too sweeping to say, that there was no poet [in England or America] who could have been of use to a beginner in 1908. The only recourse was to poetry of another language. Browning was more of a hindrance than a help, for he had gone some way, but not far enough, in discovering a contemporary idiom. And at that stage, Poe and Whitman had to be seen through French eyes. The question was still: Where do we go from Swinburne? And the answer appeared to be, nowhere.

But at the same time, the art of the theatre was being refreshed (Nazimova performed Ibsen on Broadway in 1907); and the Metropolitan Opera was in the midst of its golden age. This was the era, moreover, when American women dancers like Isadora Duncan and Ruth St. Denis were spreading a new idea of freedom in America and Europe. Alfred Stieglitz, who was to become the champion of modern painting in America, established his photograph gallery on Fifth Avenue in 1905. The Philadelphia realist painters—John Sloan, George Luks, Glackens, and others—moved to New York in 1908 and were promptly dubbed "The Ash-Can School." And scattered American publications indicated the new directions in which creative and critical winds were blowing: G. Stanley Hall's *Adolescence,* Lincoln Steffens's *The Shame of the Cities,* and Veblen's *The Theory of Business Enterprise* (all in 1904); Santayana's *The Life of Reason* (1905); Upton Sinclair's *The Jungle* (1906); Adams's *The Education of Henry Adams,* Sumner's *Folkways,* and Frank Lloyd Wright's first book on architecture (all in 1907); Gertrude Stein's *Three Lives* (1908); Van Wyck

Brooks's *The Wine of the Puritans* (1909); Lomax's *Cowboy Songs and Other Frontier Ballads* and Huneker's *Promenades of an Impressionist* (1910).

Popular reading in these years remained at its usual level of mediocrity. The center of popular interest shifted steadily westward. The sentimental New England scene of *Eben Holden* (1900) was deserted by degrees for novelized versions of the Midwest by Booth Tarkington, the Far West of Jack London and finally, for the Yukon of Rex Beach and Robert W. Service.

American poetry, in this time of almost unconscious transition, kept to tepid feeling and derivative form. Editors of the established monthly magazines determined what sort of poetic current should flow through their pages; and the use of poetry as a space filler brought in the term "magazine verse." Many of these old-line magazines were about to collapse under the pressure of more lively and sensational forces; but they collapsed with their dusty traditions intact.

The single manifestation of American poetic vigor, during these ten years, took place within a circle of young men, all of whom had been fellow students at Harvard. Henry Adams was their friend; Santayana had been their teacher. One—William Vaughan Moody—was a Westerner; and one—not a poet— was to go to the newly founded University of Chicago to teach there in the finest liberal tradition for many years; this was R o b e r t Morss Lovett. Moody achieved more fame than his friends. He succumbed, during the Cuban war, to an emotional chauvinism; but his later doubt of American power drives was clearly expressed during the war in the Philippines. His idealism was constant, and he was able to take hold of topical material. His form was not original, although it was both direct and simple. Although he wrote three dramas in verse his greatest success came in the performance of his prose plays, *The Great Divide* (1906) and *The Faith Healer* (1909).

George Cabot Lodge and Trumbull Stickney were the other poets of the group. Lodge's *Cain: A Drama* (1904) is characterized more by young energy than by any sureness of idiom; and his addiction to Tennyson marred his shorter lyrics. Stickney's talents were of quite another, and far superior, order. Born in Switzerland in 1874, and graduated from Harvard with classical honors, Stickney left Cambridge to spend seven years of study in Paris and later in Greece. A scholar of the utmost brilliance, he took the first *doctorat ès lettres* ever given to an American or Englishman by the University of Paris; and he was described after his death by a Harvard friend as "the most cultivated man I have ever known." Stickney's *Dramatic Verses* was published in 1902. A posthumous volume, *Poems* (1905), edited by George Cabot Lodge, Moody, and others, shows a poetic quality firmly his own. The melancholy of "Mnemosyne," with its subtle variation of refrain, is unforgettable; other stanzas, single lines, and complete poems must remain in the memory of the sensitive reader. Stickney broke with no traditions; but his quality is impressively pure, and, both as a man and an artist, he is the one American of his day who belongs to the world of finely tempered human beings with which, in the same period, Henry James in his last great phase was occupying himself.

Stickney died in 1904, Lodge in 1909, Moody in 1910. Moody knew Robinson in New York, where a small literary group, many of whom were interested in the theater, kept in touch with one another. Another Midwesterner, Ridgely Torrence, from Xenia,

Ohio, was also close to Robinson at this time. Torrence later was to be a pioneer dramatist of the negro theater; and, as the poetry editor of *The New Republic* during the twenties, was to give encouragement and impetus to many young poets of a younger generation than his own. Torrence's lyrics, *Hesperides* (1925) and *Poems* (1941), when belatedly published, successfully brought some of the idealism and the nostalgic music of the century's early years over into a later era.

ii

The most important forces of change, however, were beginning to function in a less idealistic scene. "Little magazines," as they were later to be labeled, were as yet in a primitive stage. A few scattered examples existed: in Ireland, where Yeats and others published *The Arrow* in connection with the activities of Dublin's Abbey Theatre; in Italy, with Gordon Craig's *The Mask;* and even in the American Midwest, after William Marion Reedy took over *The Sunday Mirror* in St. Louis, and after the *Chapbook* (1894-98) began to appear in Chicago. However, the New York versions of what was to become a literary phenomenon were linked to early examples elsewhere by the slightest of connections. Whereas these others from their beginnings were seriously devoted to the arts in one form or another, the New York publications served the arts through the operation of an almost insolent lightness; and later, with a kind of coarse hilarity. The fortnightly *M'lle New York* (1895-99), begun under the editorship of Vance Thompson, gave its readers a surface and witty account of contemporary happenings. After Huneker became an associate editor, a more serious point of view took hold: "a mild cynicism and a . . . mocking of 'sacred institutions.' " Both Thompson and Huneker managed to write as they pleased for an imagined or real "small portion of the public," and on subjects, detailed knowledge of which was lacking, in the intellectual life around them.

The case of *The Smart Set* was rather different. This monthly, subtitled "A Magazine of Cleverness," printed on pulp paper, was founded in 1890, according to one account, "as a periodical for the amusement of members of New York society." By 1908, when George Jean Nathan and H. L. Mencken began to contribute to its pages, *The Smart Set* had slipped into the position of catering to a popular taste for sordid elegance. The two young contributors shared enthusiasms for a variety of serious and "lively" arts. Their allegiances were to modern European art as a whole, and not merely to English culture; Mencken had, from the beginning, as a matter of fact, a distinct anti-English bias. They soon began to launch an unorganized campaign of jokes and sallies against entrenched American dullness—in any form, in any place. By 1913 the two young *intransigeants* with the aid of another, Willard Huntington Wright (whose chief interest at the time was French impressionist painting), had worked a remarkable transformation on their vehicle. They had early begun to publish writing, English and American, of "modernists": D. H. Lawrence, Theodore Dreiser, Ezra Pound, and others. They were constantly recommending European writers and dramatists then unheard of in the United States. Like Huneker they combined the excited interest of the amateur with a well-founded professional attitude toward literature, painting, music, and the theater. Their attacks against American moral and aesthetic assumptions came from "the right," but they paralleled and reinforced contemporary attacks from "the left." They also partially paralleled, in point of time, the journalist exposé methods of "the muckraking school," in the field of political, business, and civic reform, which S. S. McClure was sponsoring in *McClure's Magazine*. The spirit of reform was sweeping the land, but before Mencken and Nathan no voice had been raised in direct and prolonged defiance concerning the general mummification, not only of American writing, but of American mores.

Mencken, who in his early phase followed closely in Huneker's footsteps, was able, from the beginning, to express an unrepressed scorn for the ignorance and timidity of those intellectual leaders who had failed to seek out talent, or to praise whatever native genius existed. And Mencken, going straight for the moral causes underlying this national critical blankness and inertia, at an early period began to analyze the various stultifying allegiances which kept American literature from any straightforward and unbroken development. He beat the drum for more knowledge of more literatures; for a general national release from backwoods prejudices; for a culture based on genuine aesthetic principles, as opposed to any mixed moral-aesthetic approach. He worked from the underlying facts in any situation—a procedure which stemmed from his journalist training added to his basically scholarly and scientific turn of mind. The facts of American life were being suppressed because of the need, on the part of editors, publishers, clergymen, and professors, to conform to a small and already obsolete picture of American truths.

Mencken's taste in poetry was far from perfect. But he recognized vapidity and falsity when he saw them; and his hilarious reviews of bad books of verse helped to open the way toward a later more serious appreciation of good ones. And he gave—and this gift was of the utmost importance—he gave the young writers of the period a sense that in the field of literature an American listening post existed for American talent; the feeling that to love excellence was not an eccentricity; the fortifying certitude that, in spite of every evidence to the contrary, there was a living creative world elsewhere. Mencken brought out into the open the sheer pleasure of breaking rigid taboos, and, as time went on, raised this pleasure from the level of adolescent wickedness to that of mature choice and judgment, without for a moment deleting any of the life-giving spirit of comedy which so lightened critical gloom.

Mencken and Nathan became editors of *The Smart Set* in 1914, and raised it, from that date until 1923, to a magazine of first importance in the development of modern letters.

V

THE "AMERICAN RENAISSANCE," 1912-1917

THE YEAR 1912 has come to be recognized as the year in which a truly organized movement toward a new American poetry began. It was in October 1912 that Harriet Monroe began to publish, in Chicago, a little magazine entirely devoted to what the editor meticulously called, from the first, "the art of poetry." *Poetry: A Magazine of Verse,* whose role was to become historic, in its first number presented material of a mixed sort, but still of a predominantly conventional style. Miss Monroe contributed to the first issue a short parable on the subject of the fleeting fame of those kings who neglected to give over to bards the task of lending immortality to their names and exploits. She also, more realistically, printed a list of guarantors whose backing assured the magazine of at least five years of life. Why, she asked, should money and patronage flow toward the more showy arts of painting and music, while poets and their poetry were overlooked? This first number of *Poetry* published, along with the conventional verse of Arthur Davison Ficke and William Vaughan Moody, an exquisite lyric by a woman, Helen Dudley, and two poems by Ezra Pound.[1]

1. Why Chicago and why Harriet Monroe? The Midwestern city, for a generation, had been the center toward which talented young people from the surrounding prairie country had been attracted. An active and generous patronage of the arts had there come into being. The World's Columbian Exposition of 1893, and the founding of the new university had emphasized the city's growth toward culture. And this was by no means a culture detached from reality. Louis Sullivan, Frank Lloyd Wright and other architects were engaged with problems of modern steel structure as well as with highly original designs for private houses. French modernism in music was far more at home, after 1910, in the Chicago Grand Opera Company* than in the Metropolitan in New York. Miss Monroe as a girl had written and delivered the Exposition's "Columbian Ode." She was a close student of the arts, had traveled widely, and was either related to, or a close friend of, the patrons she sought out.

* The Chicago Civic Opera since 1922-23. Editor.

It is at this point that Pound enters the arena as a strong, eccentric, untiring, and seemingly inexhaustible motive force in poetry. In 1912 he was already for some years a resident of London, having left the United States "for good" in 1908, after a short and stormy attempt to adjust himself to an American academic career. Born in Idaho in 1885, he had been educated in the East. Precocious, he entered the University of Pennsylvania at fifteen and soon shifted to the status of special student, in order to follow his strong bent toward comparative literature. He spent some time in Venice, after his departure from America, in great poverty—a poverty which, however, did not prevent him from having his first collection of poems *A Lume Spento* published in a limited edition of 100. He speaks, in the *Pisan Cantos* of his starving isolation at this period; of his despairing urge, at one point, to throw the entire small lot of this first book into the Grand Canal. He went on to London, where a few friendships soon launched him in a group of artists and writers; and his *Personae* and *Exultations,* both published in 1909, received remarkably good notices in the English press. Pound's interest in comparative literature (a subject which then received little attention in academic curricula) and especially in the medieval literature of Provence, was reflected in a prose study, *The Spirit of Romance,* which appeared in 1910; by 1912 Pound had published two further books of poems: *Canzoni* (1911) and *Ripostes* (1912). *Provença* had appeared in 1910.

One of Pound's two poems, in *Poetry's* first number, was dedicated to Whistler—on the occasion of the Whistler show at the Tate Gallery in September 1912. It deserves quotation:

You also, our first great,
Had tried all ways;
Tasted and pried and worked in many fashions,
And this much gives me heart to play the game.

. . . .

You had your searches, your incertainties,
And this is good to know—for us, I mean,
Who bear the brunt of our America
And try to wrench her impulse into art.

You were not always sure, not always set
To hiding night or tuning "symphonies;"
Had not one style from birth, but tried and pried
And stretched and tampered with the media.

You and Abe Lincoln from that mass of dolts
Show us there's a chance at least of winning through.

A more awkwardly written poem cannot be imagined.
At twenty-seven Pound had yet to learn much that
he was about to preach concerning form, emphasis,
and tone. Yet in this fumbling utterance, a good deal
of Pound's authentic side—as well as much of his
nonauthentic—comes through. Here is the fanatical
artist, the born iconoclast, the American "village
atheist." The passion for great men is also apparent—along with the two sides of a nascent messianic
drive: the side that must "bear," and the side that
must "redeem." The style, moreover, is broken from
the regular beat of the iamb to the trochaic beat of
common conversational speech; and a struggle between rather affected literary procedure and the advance of natural words in their natural order, goes
on before our eyes.

Miss Monroe seems first to have heard of Pound
as an Englishman; her delight at finding him an
American is unbounded, and she proudly states that
Mr. Pound "authorizes the statement that at present
such of his poetic work as receives magazine publication in America will appear exclusively in

Poetry." This promise was soon broken (Pound appeared in *The Smart Set* as early as 1913); but Pound stayed on for years in another capacity: "[acting] as foreign correspondent of *Poetry,* keeping its readers informed of the present interests of the art in England, France and elsewhere."

The first "imagist" poem to appear in America came out promptly in *Poetry's* second issue. This was "Choricos" by the young poet Richard Aldington, later the husband of H. D. (Hilda Doolittle). *"The Imagistes,"* Miss Monroe explained, "[is] a group of ardent Hellenists who are pursuing interesting experiments in *vers libre,* trying to attain in English certain subtleties of cadence of the kind which Mallarmé and his followers have studied in French."

The link with the French symbolist poets is thus made, at the outset of the imagist movement; but it is still uncertain exactly what influences molded the early work of the group. Pound had known Miss Doolittle at the University of Pennsylvania, when her father was a professor of astronomy. There he had also met William Carlos Williams, a young medical student. Pound's own early poetic style, directly derived from Browning, was loaded with imitation-archaic language, effective at some moments but irritatingly artificial at others. Miss Doolittle now lived in London, and Pound's circle of London acquaintance included the anti-romantic "philosopher" of the arts, T. E. Hulme. Hulme's influence seems to be undeniable, in view of the fact that Pound published Hulme's *Works,* five free-verse poems, as an addendum to *Ripostes,* a volume dedicated to W. C. Williams. Also involved in the imagist situation was a growing interest in Oriental verse forms, stemming in part from Judith Gautier's translation of Chinese poetry into French. Pound, having been made

literary executor of the American orientalist, Ernest
Fenollosa, who died in 1908, had access to an extremely valuable collection of notes on, and translations of, Chinese and Japanese poetry and drama
after 1913. The influence of the French symbolists,
at this moment, was slight; whole areas of symbolist
tendency and meaning were left unexplored until a
later day. But from 1912 on, imagist tone and coloring begins to appear in Pound's own verse. *Ripostes*
announces the beginning of a more restrained and
less theatrical writer. The inversions disappear; the
language is freed from exclamations and exhortations
in the second person singular; and a new coolness
and colorlessness of surface allow Pound to deal with
contemporary material.[2]

Pound and his friends had learned from contemporary French poets and critics that vers libre demanded as much critical responsibility, on the part
of the poet himself, as poetry written in form; that
free verse should be kept, by every possible technical
means, from monotony and flaccidity. The lack of
regular meter and of rhyme should not result merely
in pieces of disguised prose. This early insistence on
the formal elements of free verse is interesting, in the
light of future developments. The early contribution
of Pound and the imagists to the establishment, in
free verse, of responsible poetic standards cannot be
overestimated. Pound's continual experiment with

2. See "A Few Notes on Imagism," *Poetry*, March 1913. Also see
"A Retrospect" in which he says: "In the spring or summer of 1912
'H. D.,' Richard Aldington and myself decided that we were agreed
upon the three principles following:
  1. Direct treatment of the 'thing' whether subjective or ob-
     jective.
  2. To use absolutely no word that does not contribute to the
     presentation.
  3. As regarding rhythm: to compose in the sequence of the
     musical phrase, not in sequence of a metronome."
Pound adds: "Naturally the second clause in the Imagist triad
was the first to be avoided." "A Stray Document" in *Make It New*
(London, Faber and Faber, 1934), p. 335.

the freer forms, from 1912 to 1916 (when the volume *Lustra* was published), finally resulted in a formal vers libre in English which was at once flexible
and severe, capable of dignity and poignance, af-
flicted with neither flabbiness nor rigidity. The imagists' admirable condensation, their attention to the
matter in hand, their complete lack of literary dilution and confusion brought into immediate notice a
clarity compared to which current "magazine verse"
seemed both soft and shabby. By the time that
formal metrics were again brought into use—by
Pound working with Eliot in the "Mauberly" period
(1920)—the years of free verse experimentation had
changed conventional English poetic procedures for
good. The former insistent iambic beat was varied;
the high pitch of poetic tone had been, as it were,
lowered; a healthy fusion between light and serious
verse had taken place. Poetry in English was again
free to be applied to any human situation, broaden-
ing out then into the freedom characteristic of high
cultures: where everything is open to the play of
mind and spirit; where there are no forbidden subjects and no proscribed methods; where poetry, again
become a natural human art, is no longer a parlor
decoration.

ii

The first years of *Poetry* were exciting ones. Not
only did Pound send Yeats, at the beginning of
Yeats' later style, to Miss Monroe, but he also introduced her to Rabindranath Tagore's translations
from the Bengali. Meanwhile, it seemed that every
hidden American quality, as well as certain American peculiarities, began to find a poetic voice. New
poetic ground was established with unbelievable
rapidity. The first American strain to appear, hitherto neglected so far as formal literature was con-

cerned, was that of the American evangelical revivalist, in Vachel Lindsay's "General Booth Enters Heaven" (*Poetry,* January 1913). Here the native fervor of the camp meeting and the religious revival was projected with its rhythms and color intact. Lindsay had revivalist blood in his veins—his mother was a Campbellite. Born in Springfield, Illinois in 1879, he studied art in Chicago and New York and did settlement work before starting out on the first of a series of long journeys on foot, through the South and later across the continent. He preached a "gospel of beauty" and tried to support himself by the sale of a pamphlet called *Rhymes to be Traded for Bread.* For several years after 1907 Lindsay repeated these tramping journeys. This endeavor to bring truth, art, and joy to rural regions was a typically eccentric American semireligious impulse; and Lindsay, in his poetry, began skilfully to combine folk rhythms with the hymn, as well as with the question and answer technique of the minstrel show. He knew and loved the color of the circus and of vaudeville—kinds of entertainment which were by this time fixed and widely diffused over the country as a whole. He was the first formal poet to strike through the country's tremendous and, at that time, still unexpended post-pioneer folk creativeness; the first to rework the railroad songs and ballads, the backcountry legends, and the neglected secular songs of the negro. Lindsay picked up ragtime syncopation, and later jazz, at its liveliest stage; and he made himself into an expert platform performer, chanting his poems to audiences with great effect. Because his sources were soundly alive, and well outside any urban or suburban taste, the impact of his earlier books on the general public was healthy in the extreme. Half-forgotten legends of the plains and prairies suddenly were brought into the consciousness of Americans who had turned away from pioneer crudity; Johnny Appleseed and "the flower-fed buffaloes" lived again, along with the almost forgotten Blackfeet and Pawnees.

Lindsay went on to celebrate the folk heroes—John Brown and Lincoln—with the more contemporary reformer John P. Altgeld; he based dreams of a classic and beautiful China on the fact of the city laundryman; and pushed the sentimental American picture of the negro back to the actual Congo. Rough and violent, picturesque and coarse American figures now received belated praise: John L. Sullivan, the prize fighter, William Jennings Bryan, Andrew Jackson, and P. T. Barnum. With an infallible instinct for the importance of these figures in "the total cultural picture," Lindsay rediscovered and revivified them. He was also quick to understand the importance of the inchoate motion pictures; his poems to Blanche Sweet and Lillian Gish early distilled the poignance of an appeal and of an influence that was to become more and more powerful in the America of the succeeding decades.

Lindsay never lost his evangelical enthusiasm; he toured the United States for many years. His later books failed to find critical support, while his popular appeal lessened as the spirit of the time drove audiences beyond appreciation of his half-visionary naïveté. He died a suicide in 1931, just before the folk material which he had done so much to uncover began to have a vogue. It is important to remember that Lindsay brought into American poetry, and very nearly singlehandedly, an unmatched richness of subject and variety of dynamics; that he broke through the shallowness and sterility of poetic subject matter as one of his beloved circus performers would break through a paper hoop.

Lindsay found his material by happy instinct; his poetry was freed more by folk patterns than by any literary innovation. Edgar Lee Masters, ten years older than Lindsay, was, on the other hand, given a method by free verse which coincided with his own nature and the nature of his material. Masters spent his youth and young manhood struggling with conventional poetic form. He was a man of forty-five in 1914—a Chicago lawyer who had written and published poems and plays under pseudonyms— when he began to write and to publish in *Reedy's Mirror* his memories of the Illinois town in which he had spent his childhood and youth. These free-verse notations, when published in 1915 under the title *Spoon River Anthology,* swung open yet another door upon neglected facts of American life: the interplay of materialism and idealism in a Midwestern town. The keynote of the poems, written in the first person in the form of self-epitaphs, is frustration—of a kind that Sherwood Anderson was soon to describe in detail and with a softer pathos. The detail here is sharp, the accent lies upon the waste of human vitality and human aspirations, and this is undoubtedly an accent weighted with remembered suffering. But the tone of the short verses is not entirely grim. Masters was able to lift the situation into a kind of nobility by contrasting misused energy with a kind of smothered gallantry. It is not entirely without a hint of nostalgia that he looks back upon these thin, baffled, sour lives kept from full knowledge of themselves and others by false allegiances, ignorance, and bigotry; and by the fear and deception resultant upon the rigidity of moral standards. A fiber of energy runs through these portraits; they are neither mawkish nor cynical.

Many readers responded to the truth and the succinct method of *Spoon River*. In spite of a minority that condemned it as "sensational" the book became the first best seller of the "poetic Renaissance." Masters never succeeded in equaling either the power or the appeal of this book in his later writing; and a shadow of bitterness and of rather small-minded iconoclasm clouds his many subsequent books. *Spoon River,* however, bears the mark of the difficulties that shaped it—difficulties which made it important for more than its own day.

A third Midwestern talent, basically quite different from that of either Masters or Lindsay, although superficially close to both, was that of Carl Sandburg. Born in 1878 in Galesburg, Illinois, of Swedish immigrant parentage, he spent his youth as an untrained worker in many haphazard jobs, served in Puerto Rico during the Spanish-American War, and later entered Lombard College in Galesburg. On leaving college, he became a salesman and newspaperman in Chicago. In 1904 he had printed a pamphlet of twenty-two poems. Ten years later "Chicago Poems," a free-verse group, appeared in *Poetry.* Here realism in the Whitman vein was tempered with a kind of Scandinavian mysticism. Sandburg added to the effects of the free-verse realists by writing in common speech, in coarse vernacular, in current slang—a procedure more or less avoided by Lindsay and totally lacking in Masters. Sandburg also broadened the field by his descriptions of scenes of industry: of the packing houses, the mills, and the factories at the outskirts of the cities, by which the cities were fed and of which the cities were somewhat ashamed. And this industrial grime, stench, grinding, shriek, and clatter is celebrated by Sandburg, as well as described.

Sandburg later wrote in *Cornhuskers* (1918), of the enormous panorama of the Western farmlands—a turn of attention which brought out the moods of delicacy of which he was capable. He wrote in alternating impressionist and heroic terms, not only of the sweeping land, but of the courage, and the constant yet restless purpose, of the men who cultivated it with their machines. Later Sandburg who, like Lindsay, had in him a streak of the wandering bard, applied his attention to the American folk song, gathering together examples of many kinds in his *American Song Bag* (1927). Sandburg's chief insight was his understanding that folk material never ceases to be produced—that it flows and renews itself continually in popular forms and in common speech. His chief fault was his romantic insistence on the complete and all-embracing worth of this folk material. As time went on his praise of the folk quality reached a point where, as in *The People Yes* (1936), it became a form of flattery. His tribute to the inexhaustible power resident in the common man, his recognition of indestructible human virtues layered between the waste, the disorder and violence of an industrial society, were well-founded. His celebration of these truths, however, became increasingly diffuse and sentimental as time went on. Sandburg's poetry, at its worst, shows the effects of journalism—in the tendency to exploit matters for news or shock value. This tendency has helped to make him one of the most popular poetic figures of the time; but his early poems remain his best and most sincere ones.

iii

New freedoms in subject and treatment continued to widen the American poetic horizon. Americans were beginning to produce their own brand of impressionism. But this impressionism lacked background; it had not grown by slow stages, but had burst into being overnight. A shift of sensibility had been marked by a change in form, but both form and sensibility were still free-floating—without definite roots. A young and growing art must have some liaison with convention. Some feeling for rule and order must exist. If the American poetic Renaissance had succeeded only in establishing a set of American experimentalists, without an accompanying group of formalists, its successes would have been shallow, indeterminate, and fleeting. We have seen to what an extent the imagists insisted on purity of direction and economy of means; their struggle to keep these ends important was, in fact, just beginning. At this time an American poet came into view whose form, although conventional, was original enough to further widen and diversify the American poetic scene. He was Robert Frost, whose first book of poems, *A Boy's Will*, was published in London in 1913.

Frost, born in San Francisco in 1875, was brought back as a boy to his family's native New England by his widowed mother. He graduated from high school in the industrial city of Lawrence, Massachusetts, and, after his marriage in 1895, entered Harvard College for a stay of two years. His early poetry found no favor with magazine editors, and he determined, after spending his young manhood as a teacher and farmer in New Hampshire, to try his luck in England. Once in England, he made friends among the poets who called themselves "Georgian." He also met Pound, who felt "reality" in him.

Frost's early poems have a simple, unforced lyric charm; they seem to have been written as naturally and effortlessly as breathing. Frost, also from the first, presented a contrast to Robinson by being less literary and closer to the soil than his fellow New Englander. Frost is "a countryman." He has a deep love for natural things, for things of field and pasture, for bird, flower, weed, and tree; and for the motions and rhythms attendant upon man's age-old cultivation of the land—the rhythm of sowing and reaping in recurring seedtime and harvest. Frost also sees with great clearness the wayward and frustrating elements which run counter to nature's abundance and man's efforts on nature's behalf and on his own. His sympathy with the stray, the unused, and the overlooked gives his best poetry poignance and pathos. What he cannot bear to contemplate at length are the evidences that veins of evil run deeply through the natural scene.

North of Boston, published in England with success in 1914, achieved American acclaim the following year. The poems in *North of Boston* are for the most part written in isolated dramatic scenes, or else in the dramatic monologue Browning had done so much to develop. In these episodes Frost broke through all stock ideas concerning New England country living into the tragedy and eccentric comedy of a countryside still bound to obsolete and degenerating custom. He described a dying region's ingrown life; its joys and fears; its stubborn strength still opposed to decay; its terrors and stratagems; its common sense and its groundwork of human dignity. Here is a countryside still lit by lamps and lanterns, still measured by the slow pace of a man's walk or a horse's run. Here is Yankee talk made an integral part of the drama. To use a speech so close to patois, without slipping over into the dangers of actual dialect, was in itself an achievement. Frost was able, moreover, to keep his incidents dramatic, although his material is continually working against this intensification toward a lower level, that of the sentimental-colloquial.

In *North of Boston* Frost briefly possessed himself of a humane realism and insight which he was never quite able to repeat. And even here he deleted facts which would have broken a frame he wished to keep intact, the frame of a folk culture at its dead end when the loneliness of rural isolation is bringing madness, obsession, and a collapse of the will to people whose only weapons are a shrewd humor and calculation. In reality, this dead end had been broken by industrialization; but Frost skirts the problem of the mills and of a new immigrant population. By so doing he is able, at first, to crystallize his drama. By continuing to eliminate these facts he finally leaves the entire situation dangling and incomplete.[3]

Frost's later work never completely realized the tragic power that *North of Boston* promised. In *West Running Brook* (1928) he began to play with the role of self-conscious homespun philosopher. He began to give reasons for his innate, countryman's conservatism, and not only reasons, but arguments which were half-apologies. His own native shrewdness began to get the upper hand; and, although his lyrical gift remained very nearly untouched, he began to shift his sympathy, with almost imperceptible slowness, away from wildness and unpredictability, toward the weather-safe side of existence. "Let what will be, be" became his creed; he reinforced this stoicism, which in itself had a certain dignity, with an active insistence upon burrowing under and dig-

---

3. Frost's single recognition of New England industrialization occurs in his poem "A Lone Striker."

ging safely in. We see in this attitude the ancient conservatism of the man who depends upon the earth for his living; but Frost's later work seems to base its skepticism less upon intelligent common sense than upon unthinking timidity. The appeal Frost made to large numbers of people began to be attached to a series of refusals rather than to a set of affirmations. He stopped exploring the frightening outside—and the heights and depths come into his later work only in a repressed, and therefore negative and melancholy, way.

But it is difficult to imagine the American poetry of our time without the figure of Frost being deeply involved in it from the start. His early themes were indeed real, with a reality for which American expression was starved, and lacking which it would not have achieved, in the following restless years, full balance. Frost's use of understatement and of ellipsis, both emotional and stylistic, helped to bring the lyric and the short dramatic poem written in English onto a level where they could deal easily with everyday matters; and the younger poets learned from him. His moments of vision, expressed on this level, take on an added poignance; the ordinary event is given an unexpected turn, the universal flashes through.

Frost's career has another importance to the America of his time. He restored to a large audience the concept of The Bard—a more acceptable concept than that of The Seer to a society in transition. His insistence on uniting his vocation with his avocations, on living according to his beliefs and within his means—as teacher, farmer, and poet—reconstituted a simple and self-controlled poetic character which had been attractive to the middle class since the Victorian era. He advocated none but the simplest virtues and expressed the most graspable ideas. That he early began to slip over, by almost imperceptible degrees, from bitter portrayals of rural facts into a romantic nostalgia for a vanished way of life, his admirers refused to acknowledge. Frost's final role— that of the inspired purveyor of timeless and granitic wisdom—has proved acceptable to all concerned, including the poet himself. The bearded bards of the schoolbooks now have a modern counterpart.

Frost's later poems indicate that he knows more than he ever allows himself to say. He has come to hold so tightly to his "views" that they at last have very nearly wiped out his vision.

VI

VERS LIBRE AND AVANT-GARDE, 1913-1918

AMERICAN POETRY, from 1914 to the date of
America's entry into the war in April 1917, developed schools and tendencies in a remarkably short
space of time. The allover picture can be puzzling
if two large trends are not described at once.

In the first place, free verse (vers libre) became
a separate movement, which soon split into "formal"
and "popular" manifestations.

In the second place, a split occurred in all fields,
between more conventional and more experimental
poetic expression.

Pound was characteristically involved in the events
which helped to bring about a marked division between popular and formal free verse. In London in
1913, he had met Amy Lowell, a New Englander of
established family and fortune, and the sister of
Abbott Lawrence Lowell, then president of Harvard
University. Miss Lowell's first book, *A Dome of
Many Colored Glass*, published in 1912, was pre-
vailingly sentimental, and bound over to the tone
and manner of Tennyson and Keats. Her second
volume, *Sword Blades and Poppy Seeds* (1914),
published after her meeting with the imagists, was
completely different in method and material. Her
publishers advertised Miss Lowell as "the foremost
member of the Imagists," and placed her at the head
of a list which included Yeats, Ford Madox Ford
(Hueffer), and Pound himself. Pound promptly
scotched this attempt to take over, by writing Miss
Lowell a stern letter on the ridiculous presumption
of her publisher's claims. Imagism, he insisted, was

built upon a core of form, and it was to this core
that American and English poets worthy of the name
Imagist, must adhere. Otherwise, Pound stated, the
American poetic renaissance would consist of nothing
but an undisciplined expression of experience and
emotion: a kind of expression which had nothing to
do with the basic disciplines of art. Miss Lowell,
undeterred by Pound's chiding, energetically pursued
her own course. She produced poems in quantity,
written in what she came to term "polyphonous
prose." "A demon saleswoman," in the words of
Eliot, she spread the gospel of free verse on the
lecture platform and in her anthologies; and formed
her own clique of admirers.[1] "Free verse," of her own
particular brand, under her aegis, began to enroll
practitioners. It not only became popular itself, but
it invaded other popular fields, showing up in the
style of advertisements and that of those newspaper
feature writers who were beginning to call themselves
"columnists." Miss Lowell's "school" was later described by Pound as "Amygism."

Just as Pound was right in his insistence that a
young aesthetic movement cannot give in to vulgar-
ization of its aims and methods, so were the bolder
experimenters of the time right in their more or less
instinctive pursuit of variety and individuality. In
any growing art, every line must be explored to its
end; all manner of temperaments and of stylistic
variation must be given room. The fact that a change
in direction was overdue accounts in part for the
suddenness of the separation of the more serious and
formal line, into conventional and experimental

---

1. Pound edited *Des Imagistes,* an anthology, in 1914. Miss
Lowell, breaking with Pound's "leadership," edited three anthologies,
entitled *Some Imagist Poets,* in 1915, 1916, and 1917 respectively.

groups. Procedures destructive to the old had to be improvised along with procedures of renewal, restoration and replacement.

In France, from about 1870 on, poetry, which up to that time had developed according to a more or less unbroken convention, had been split (by Rimbaud) into two tendencies: the formal, and the experimental or *avant-garde*. Albert Thibaudet, in his history of French literature (Paris, 1936), has described this division, which the symbolists of the 1880's enlarged and made permanent:

> The Romantic and Parnassian revolutions had as their objective conquest and organization, and a stable condition of poetry—liberty, but liberty within limits. But Symbolism habituated literature to the idea of an indefinite revolution—to an artistic *blanquisme*, to youth's right and duty to jostle the preceding generation while rushing toward an absolute. . . . Literature divided itself into normal literature and literature of the advance guard. The Symbolist revolution—the last up to now—is perhaps the absolute last, because it incorporated the motif of chronic revolution into literature's normal state.

It was not necessary, therefore, for the more experimental side of American poetry, in its early stages, to operate completely without background or examples. Poets were able to turn their attention to European developments in the arts, and there to find both confirmation and inspiration. It is necessary at this point to indicate the nature and scope of European prewar experiment, in order to understand much of the American experiment, both before the war and thereafter.

A new spirit had recently taken hold of French painting and poetry. Compared to the spirit of impressionism, it was harder, more formal and more abstract; it was strongly colored by primitive elements which were both foreign and violent. The exhibition of *Les Fauves* in Paris in 1905, had displayed this spirit, caught from Cézanne, Van Gogh, and Gauguin. The interest of French painters in African primitive art dates from the same period.[2] The painters whose chief interest was an analysis of natural forms down to basic structure, were later called "Post-Impressionists" by Roger Fry. By 1910 the more abstract members of the group were calling themselves "Cubists."

But perhaps the most pervasive aesthetic influence in these prewar years, in France and England, was that of the *Ballet Russe* under Sergei Diaghilev (1872-1929). Diaghilev, an amateur-connoisseur of the arts in general, left St. Petersburg for Paris in 1906, and there continued his career as organizer and impresario of Russian painting and music. He formed, in 1909, with the aid of Bakst and others, a ballet company whose Parisian season in the same year was a sensational success. In 1910 Stravinsky's original and exotic *Fire Bird* was added to the repertoire. Stravinsky's *Petrouchka* appeared in 1911. In 1912 Nijinsky appeared in his own rather shocking choreographic arrangement of Debussy's *L'Après-midi d'un faune*. The greatest "scandal," however, centered, in 1913, around the savage rhythms of Stravinsky's *Le sacre du printemps*. This ballet, which projected a sacrificial ritual of pagan Russia, was received, by audiences in Paris and London, with the utmost derision. But it made its mark upon the times and heralded many experiments in the primitive to come.

Postimpressionism in painting came to the United States in 1913 with the "Armory Show"; the *Ballet*

---

2. Maurice de Vlaminck claims, in his memoirs *Portrait avant décès* (Paris, Flammarion, 1943) that he was the first to draw the attention of his friends Derain, Picasso, and Apollinaire, in 1905, to the African masks and *fétiches* from the Ivory Coast, which he had come upon in sailors' cafés outside Paris.

Russe made an American tour in 1915. The impact of the Armory Show was sharp and immediate. News of its "shocking" innovations was spread more by ridicule than by praise; but the news spread, and the pictures were reproduced in Sunday supplements throughout the nation. In 1914 a spirit of extreme modernism showed up in the first numbers of *The Little Review* published in Chicago under the editorship of Margaret Anderson.

The Little Review, at its first appearance, was distinguished more by an adolescent *Schwärmerei* than by any definite program. Editorially, Miss Anderson defined the magazine's direction: it was to be "a magazine that believes in Life for Art's sake, in the individual rather than an Incomplete people . . . a magazine written for intelligent people who can feel; whose philosophy is Applied Anarchism, whose policy is a Will to the Splendor of Life." All this added up, in the early issues, to little more than fulsome praise of Mary Garden, who had been appearing with the Chicago Civic Opera Company since 1910, and of other romantic artistic personalities. The true importance of *The Little Review* as a vehicle of *avant-garde* literature began in 1917, again under the influence (as "foreign editor") of the ubiquitous Pound.

Chicago now had its more conservative *Poetry* and its experimental *Little Review.* New York City, in 1915, produced its own little magazine of an experimental order. *Others,* under the editorship of Alfred Kreymborg, furnished an outlet for the publication of those poets who had not appeared, or had appeared infrequently, in *Poetry* because of Miss Monroe's inherent dislike of poetry which ultimately "did not make sense." A new, and definitely experimental, group formed itself around this new center.

These experimentalists included Marianne Moore, William Carlos Williams, Mina Loy, and Wallace Stevens. Owing to lack of funds, *Others* was published irregularly after 1916, and disappeared in 1919. Its spirit, however, was later to be caught up and enlarged.

ii

It is apparent, in looking back over the poetry published by these early *avant-garde* little magazines, that much of the impulse shared by their contributors was insecurely based and prematurely projected. Much of the writing was imitative. Harsh and violent influences were being absorbed from all sides, and the result was often confusion between the contributors' native endowments and the use to which these were put. But through this confusion ran a thread of actual creative force, behind which was a real creative need. American art has always been characterized by the sudden emergence of temperaments developed far beyond their place and time. Americans are not a homogenous people and American creativeness cannot, therefore, proceed in an orderly fashion. The history of the early American *avant-garde,* which came into being before 1918, stands as proof of this fact. Out of the dozens of writers attracted to the new poetic media, only five or six were equipped, intellectually or temperamentally, to understand the possibilities which were opening before them, and to manipulate them with ease.

An event which came in for a good deal of the period's publicity-through-ridicule, was the publication, in 1914, of a small collection of poems, privately printed in New York by a publisher who called himself "Claire Marie." This book was *Tender Buttons* by Gertrude Stein and the publisher was Donald Evans, a young newspaperman who wrote experimental verse of a rather interesting kind. The influence of *Tender Buttons,* as its contents were reprinted and facetiously commented on in the press by columnists and others, became widespread. Miss Stein was a Californian who had lived for years in Paris. She had studied under Münsterberg at Harvard and had experimented with automatic writing in his classes. These experiments were undoubtedly the underlying factor beneath Miss Stein's "portraits" of her friends and other notes, put down in "poetic prose," although Miss Stein never admitted any such connection. Her poems, which sometimes consisted only of a sentence or two, were often delightful: her sense of style, her feeling for words, and her peculiar wit combined to make them unforgettable—in spite of their total lack of logical "meaning." Miss Stein was the friend of the group of cubist painters in Paris, headed by Picasso and Juan Gris. The connection between modern poetry and modern painting becomes definite in her work. It is interesting to note that 1914 was the year of the publication of James Joyce's *Dubliners,* stories in which Joyce was still definitely tied to the more formal nineteenth-century French tradition of fiction. Therefore, Miss Stein's experiments, in which logical meaning is definitely eliminated, are the first of the kind to reach America and to be caught up by the poetic experimentalists who were then functioning.

Some of the tenets of the symbolist theory were thus put into active practice before very much critical background had formed in English. This lack of general critical and theoretic background was a peculiarity of the forming experimental school. Much was done by instinct; and this more or less unguided operation of talent accounts for some of the freshness, as well as for some of the faults, of American *avant-garde* writing at its beginnings.

Three distinguished talents, in the experimental field, should be here examined—those of Wallace Stevens, Marianne Moore, and William Carlos Williams. Williams, of course, had his close connection with Pound and Hilda Doolittle: all three had been students together at the University of Pennsylvania and had kept in touch with each other throughout the years by correspondence. Born in 1883, Williams became a doctor in Rutherford, New Jersey, his birthplace. His father was an Englishman, and his mother a Puerto Rican of Basque and Spanish-Jewish descent. After studying in Europe, he published his first small volume in 1909. This was followed by *The Tempers* (1913), published in London with Pound's aid. Williams' early poems exhibited a formal lyricism; and although he later turned away from this formality, his unerring ear for language and his fine discretion and economy are securely based upon it. Williams instinctively turned to the facts of his everyday life for poetic material; he distilled from these facts, over the years, a body of work remarkable for its clarity of outline and consistency of purpose. He continued to reflect the life he knew—"life along the Passaic"—by means of a free verse which never became either mechanical or, in spite of his often brutal frankness, coarsened or blurred. His point of view was at once anarchic and humane; but his straightforward anger at injustice always remained that of the detached observer. If at times he seemed to lack depth, to write like a person whose unconscious motives are not entirely open to, or operable by, his conscious personality, his sense of the tragic in everyday life is everywhere evident.

In direct contrast to Williams with his infallible instinct toward the heart of the commonplace, his ease with the vernacular, and his openness to every-

day events, Wallace Stevens, from the beginning, exhibited traits which linked him not only with impressionism, but with some of the more faded and
artificial attributes of English *fin-de-siècle* aestheti-
cism. Stevens, born in 1879 in Pennsylvania, is part-
ly of Pennsylvania Dutch stock. He studied law in
New York after leaving Harvard, and early became
associated with the Hartford Accident and Indemnity
Company. Miss Monroe published poems of his in
1914, and later honored him with an award. He
later appeared in *Others* and in a number of little
magazines. His contact with Bohemian circles was
rather brief—he visited the *salon* of Mabel Dodge,
an early patroness of the arts, and knew the Kreymborg group; but his withdrawal to Hartford cut these
associations short.

Stevens presents, for the greater part of his career,
the picture of a man whose professional and poetic
aspects are so markedly divided that they touch only
because they are part of the same personality. This
division tended to alienate Stevens, until his later
years, from the cruder aspects of reality. His early
poetry moves almost exclusively on levels where the
imaginative faculty may express itself by means of
an atmosphere of luxury and exotic beauty. His
early tropical backgrounds are filled with objects
which, even when natural, have an air of being artifacts; and he arranges his *décor* with all the exquisite
discrimination of a connoisseur. All this moved toward preciosity; it was Stevens' dramatic sense which
saved him from the affectation by which he was continually threatened. His sense of form and his gifts
of language were extraordinary; these, added to his
dramatic power, which produced many moments of
tension—"The Emperor of Ice Cream" is an example
of such a moment—lifted his work from the realm of

the arabesque and the rococo. However, his affiliation with impressionism is marked; his fanciful titles derive very probably from Debussy's taste for such titles—and Stevens' relation to impressionist painting, in his use of color and texture, is also clear.

The work of Williams and of Stevens constitutes two long lines of creativeness and of influence which run through more than thirty years of American poetry. Their later phases must be dealt with in their place. The same length of creative line is present in the work of Marianne Moore who was born in 1887. Miss Moore's idiosyncracies were, from the beginning of her career, her own. She combined, in an odd but striking fashion, the attributes of the naturalist with those of a philosophic moralist. Her insight often struck close to the heart of things; she could delineate with the precision of a miniaturist, and subsequently raise the most curious and fine of her pictures to a higher power, by relating them directly to abstract truth. Her form, based on a syllabic line, with hidden and unaccented rhymes, was also completely her own. Her sense of language was firmly attached to the logical sequences of prose; she often gained an effect—always in imaginative terms—by seeming to clinch an argument. Her sense of color and of music became more marked as time went on; the poems of her middle period are filled with a dazzling array of detail which exists in her earlier work only as occasional touches. Her habit of using quotations not as illustrations, but as a means to extend and complete a poem's original intentions—her habit of "hybrid composition," as she called it—never became eccentric but, on the contrary, often gave her composition an added dimension of wit.

Miss Moore's first collection, *Poems,* was published in pamphlet form by the Egoist Press in London in 1921. This London press was an adjunct of the fortnightly *The Egoist*, which in 1914 superseded the feminist *The New Freewoman* and became, under the editorship of Harriet Shaw Weaver, a vehicle less of feminism than of Pound's ideas. Pound was now furnished with a solid foundation for his unending activities as writer, *impresario*, and showman. He was also closely connected with the brief establishment, in June and July of 1914, of the magazine *Blast* ("The Review of the Great English Vortex"). Wyndham Lewis edited *Blast*, but he has acknowledged that the term "vortex," as well as many of the shock tactics of this short-lived effort to awaken the British public to a violent new aesthetic, came from Pound. *Blast's* violence extended to its typography— in English it was the first application of advertising techniques to literature; Lewis and Pound also used the techniques of the literary manifesto, learned from Marinetti and the futurists. *The Egoist* went on in a quieter way to advance the "new spirit." In its pages a critical background to modernism's continuous creative display began to be built up, by degrees.

VII

POSTWAR ACHIEVEMENT, 1917-1930

THE HISTORY of American poetry, from 1917 to
the present, seems to fall neatly into decades. It is
important to realize that this neatness is largely due
to our present shortness of perspective; later periods
will be able to see more cohesion and relevance
within the period as a whole. There is no doubt,
however, that the postwar decade of the twenties
opened more possibilities in the American arts and
broke up more social and moral pressures than any
comparable period of ten years, in the past.

The new aesthetic freedom was part of a new
moral freedom. The period was one of general "de-
compression." America broke away with startling
suddenness from a set of oppressive and outmoded
ruling ideas; people began to find new uses for their
surplus energy. They began to learn how to play.
They began to express themselves as individuals, to
enjoy the new freedoms offered them by the machine;
a general Bohemianization of the middle class began.
If this movement toward a more civilized and less
fundamentalist point of view was often accompanied
by silliness and violence, it was, nevertheless, a
movement in the right direction: toward general enlightenment and away from hampering provincial
taboos.

Two needs now showed up in the rapidly changing
aesthetic picture. The first was the need for a stable
and informed criticism. So far as poetry was concerned, the creative side of the movement had shot
ahead with very little accompanying critical background; the first critical developments were either

highly impressionistic or marked by a journalistic emphasis upon the flashy and the popular. Again, a purely social point of view activated many of the early critics. This social form of thinking and feeling was, at the time, both pertinent and high-minded. But it was a materialistic standpoint, and therefore one upon which a broad and deep aesthetic could not be built. What is likely to occur whenever social thinking is linked too closely with the motives of art, showed up early in the short career of *The Seven Arts,* a monthly founded in 1916 by James Oppenheim, Waldo Frank, and Van Wyck Brooks. These editors were interested in analyzing American culture as a whole; poetry was caught up into this analysis and treated not so much as a separate art, but as a part of a general "liberal" coming of age of the American social conscience. That this interest, being partial, had no real strength or validity, was proved before the magazine ceased publication under war pressures.

The second and, at the time, more crucial need was the need for literature in general to free itself from that last and rear-guard action of bigotry which showed up as censorship. Prose literature, and particularly the novel, was more closely involved in this struggle than poetry; but it is important to remember that this conflict between opposed forces was a severe and prolonged one, and that final freedom from the powers of "comstockery" was won only by a determined and planned strategy on the part of writers, editors, and intellectuals at large (of whom Mencken turned out to be a vigorous leader).

ii

For a time America's entrance into the war tended to hinder and baffle any open expression of opinion and ideas. In England in 1914, a new and romantic poetic *genre* came into being with Rupert Brooke's sonnets written at the outbreak of hostilities. Brooke was a Georgian poet, although his talent took certain modern turns in choice of material and treatment. His war sonnets, however, were in a direct line with Kiplingesque romantic imperialism. "War poetry" of this idealist and sentimental kind was to have the briefest of existences; the tragic and realistic works of Siegfried Sassoon, Wilfred Owen, Edmund Blunden, and others were shortly to appear and to abolish it for good. Nevertheless, war poetry was produced in quantity for a time in the United States; even *Poetry* let down critical barriers on its behalf.

The main line of events now shifts to England. The years just before the war, and the war years, were those in which Pound's own talents reached their most ordered and interesting point. In *Cathay* (1915), a set of translations and "renderings" from the Fenollosa manuscripts, Pound for the first time hit upon a feasible "middle style." His work with Yeats, during the period from 1912 to 1916, had resulted in mutual benefit. Yeats' later style, announced in *Responsibilities* (1914), was without doubt influenced by both the Fenollosa material and by Pound's imagist insistence on clarity of thought and simplicity of means; and the later Yeatsian manner was about to become widely influential with a young poetic generation. Modern American poetry, as well as all poetry written in English, was to be crucially affected, from this point on, by this Anglo-Irishman, as well as by Pound acting in close collaboration with an American compatriot also at the time resident in London.

It was in 1914 that Pound first came upon, and immediately recognized, the quality of the writing and of the intelligence of a young American then doing graduate work at Merton College, Oxford. Pound writes, in September 1914, to Harriet Monroe: "I was jolly well right about Eliot. He has sent in the best poem I have yet seen from an American. *Pray God it be not a single and unique success.* . . . He is the only American I know of who has made what I call adequate preparation for writing. He has actually trained *and* modernized himself *on his own*. The rest of the *promising young* have done one or the other, but never both." To Mencken, for whom he was also serving as a "foreign advisor," Pound writes (October 1914), "very nicely drawn" of Eliot's "Portrait of a Lady." In the same month, Pound sends "The Love Song of J. Alfred Prufrock" to Miss Monroe, who printed it in the June 1915 issue of *Poetry*.

Pound published his *Catholic Anthology* (1915) with the basic intention, as he remarked at the time, of getting a group of Eliot's poems into print as quickly as possible. Eliot's first small volume, *Prufrock, and Other Observations,* was published in 1917 by the Egoist Press; and its effect upon a small "advanced" public was immediate. Here the materials and methods chosen by the young American in order to modernize himself were clearly apparent. He had been able to establish contact with French nineteenth-century experiment as no poet writing in English, up to that time, had succeeded in doing— and that by absorbing the manner, and some of the matter, of Jules Laforgue. He had made the discovery, as he later stated, that Laforgue's poetry was "free verse in much the same way that the later verse of Shakespeare, Webster and Tourneur is free verse. . . . My own verse is, so far as I can judge, nearer to the original meaning of *vers libre* than is any [of certain other types]: at least, the form in which I began to write, in 1908 or 1909, was directly drawn from the study of Laforgue together with the later Elizabethan drama; and I do not know anyone who started from exactly that point."[1]

We find in Eliot, therefore, a style and a tone completely free from those mannerisms of late nineteenth-century English poetry which had been such a stumbling block to Pound. Pound was forced to discover modernity. Eliot was modern from the beginning.

Born in 1888 into a St. Louis family with distinguished New England forbears, Thomas Stearns Eliot entered Harvard in 1906, where he studied under Irving Babbitt and George Santayana. Completing his college course in three years, he spent a year in the Graduate School and one at the Sorbonne, reading French literature and philosophy. He then returned to Harvard, "extending his study of metaphysics, logic and psychology to include Indic philology and Sanskrit." He was granted a traveling fellowship in 1914, and was in Germany during the summer of the outbreak of the war. He spent the following winter at Merton College, Oxford, reading Greek philosophy; and it was at this time, as we have seen, that he first came to Pound's attention. His early poems were published not only in *Poetry* but in Wyndham Lewis' *Blast*. After teaching briefly at the Highgate School near London, he entered Lloyd's Bank. He became assistant editor of *The Egoist* in 1917 and was a frequent contributor, during 1919 to 1921, to *The Atheneum* under Middleton Murry's editorship. In 1923 he became editor of *The Criterion*, a post he held until the end of the thirties. In 1927, "as a result of his growing interest in the English Church and State," he became a British subject.

---

1. Eliot in the Preface to *Selected Poems of Ezra Pound*, p. viii.

Eliot's chief interest, in the early days of the English (and American) poetry revival, was to work through to some manner of poetic expression which would give him freedom to examine and to interpret the material and spiritual condition of the complex transitional scene in which he found himself: in his own words, "to be able to see [as a poet] beneath both beauty and ugliness: to see the boredom, the horror and the glory." Temperamentally Eliot was very nearly Pound's exact opposite. He acted as a counterbalance to the older man's tendencies toward shrillness and shallowness. Eliot had learned from Laforgue, Corbière, and others, as Pound and Yeats had learned from Chinese and Japanese poetry and drama, that modern sensibility, which suspects the grandiose and the heroic, may yet express intense feeling by oblique means. It was not Eliot's wish to lighten poetry's burden, but rather in some manner to shift and disguise it, so that the imagination could be applied to the ordinary contemporary scene without the use of outworn and inflated stylistic trappings. Jules Laforgue (1860-1887) in his short career had brought into French poetry, at symbolism's most serious and humorless stage, an unexpected and refreshing ironic lightness and sense of parody. "He used argot," says a French critic, "he mingled despair with humor; he mixed *genres* and epochs, writing of Hamlet in nineteenth-century terms; and opened the eyes of certain French poets of the first order to the possibility of liberation through irony."

We find very nearly the complete list of these means and attributes in the early Eliot. "Prufrock" and "Portrait of a Lady" translate Laforgue into Eliot's terms; "Rhapsody on a Windy Night," "Preludes," and "Hysteria" are almost pure Laforgue.

By 1920, the year in which his second volume, *Poems,* was published, Eliot had submitted to other influences, which had pulled him back to more regular form. Pound had introduced him to Gautier's *Emaux et camées*—"a book I had hitherto overlooked." In *Polite Essays* (1937), Pound characteristically describes the decision made, at this period, by Eliot and himself:

At a particular date in a particular room, two authors, neither engaged in picking one another's pockets, decided that the dilution of *vers libre,* Amygism, Lee Masterism, general floppiness, had gone too far and that some countercurrent must be set going. Parallel situation centuries ago in China. Remedy prescribed *Emaux et Camées* (or the Bay State Hymn Book). Rhyme and regular strophes. Results: poems in Mr. Eliot's *second* volume, not contained in . . . "Prufrock" . . . also "H. S. Mauberly." Divergence later.

Eliot's irony in *Poems* is heavily weighted with bitterness; and he does not spare himself, but includes a self-mocking portrait, written in French, with a title borrowed from Corbière: "Mélange adultère de tout." In this volume Eliot's dramatic gift is crystallized for the first time. The character of Sweeney emerges—that symbol of the flesh—and there is an acid portrait of naïve American culture hunters in "Lune de miel." The poem "Whispers of Immortality" introduces and dramatizes the figures of Donne and Webster: an introduction which was to have wide reverberations in the poetry of Eliot's imitators during the coming years.

Eliot's *Poems* is an indictment of the age—an indictment with little pity or sympathy. Pound's "Hugh Selwyn Mauberly" (1920) presents a concentrated survey of Pound's London career as well as a dire criticism of postwar life. Written with comparative straightforwardness in stanzas brilliantly compressed, Mauberly appears as a minor poet who

is Pound and yet not Pound and who turns, at the
end, toward some refuge in the tropic seas. Pound
himself was about to leave London for Paris, and
finally, in 1925, for Rapallo, where he was to spend
a long series of increasingly embittered and obsessive
years. "Mauberly," not published in America until
1926 (in *Personae*) had a belated influence upon
American writing. From this point on, the importance of Eliot was to increase, while that of Pound
declined.

iii

Eliot's first book of essays, *The Sacred Wood*
(1920), stands as a landmark in the history of modern literary criticism. Here, for the first time in English, poetry of a variety of periods was subjected to
close scrutiny and analysis, always in *poetic terms,*
though backed up by formidable general scholarship.
Eliot now began to accompany the development of
his own poetry with a series of critical comments on
the poetry of many different eras, in many different
languages. Unlike Pound, who never worked out the
principles of his poetic belief and procedure with any
orderly care, and whose demand for a continually
renewed *originality* on the part of the writers of his
time finally became rather empty and meaningless,
Eliot proceeded, with great seriousness and patience,
to break the reputation of one poet after another out
of the bondage of mere scholarship, to examine
minutely their quality, to draw conclusions from their
practice. In thus restoring life and energy to poets
and dramatists overlooked, ignored, and neglected by
nineteenth-century taste, he immensely enriched the
modern field. Because of Eliot's critical contribu-
tions, the wilder oscillations of modern taste and
sensibility were given standards by which to steady
themselves; and modern poetry was furnished with

an historical perspective. The chief figures to emerge from the darkness which had so long surrounded them were Jonson, Blake, and Dante. Later Eliot thoroughly analyzed the quality and greatness of Donne and Baudelaire. The English "metaphysicals" of the seventeenth century were also brought into modern focus. Eliot not only defined their quality in his 1921 essay, *The Metaphysical Poets,* but, connecting them with Laforgue and Corbière, indicated forcefully what English poetry had lost by developing away from their sort of intensity.

The importance of the influence of Eliot's early criticism cannot be overestimated. Poets began to see a way through the forest of schools and various influences imposed upon them by their education. One clarification of Eliot's was recognized as of inestimable value—his remarks that "honest criticism and sensitive appreciation are directed not upon the poet but the poetry." A whole new approach to literature was thus defined. The distortions of the romantic critical standards, as well as dry-as-dust philological methods, began to fall into place, under the light of this wider view—the view, it is important to remember, of a poet who was putting his findings into actual practice. Eliot armed a new generation with a new arsenal of insights and intimations; he provided an impetus toward further study and research. If his influence brought into American poetry a touch of eclecticism, the restorative strength of his ideas at the same time opened the way toward a thorough canvassing of values, and emphasized the importance of rejecting the undirected and the formless. At a moment when the idea of freedom was being applied unthinkingly in many quarters of art and life, Eliot's example checked and dammed a creative stream which otherwise might have quickly spent and exhausted its energy.

In America, the beginning publication (January 1920) of *The Dial,* a monthly review of literature and the arts, under the editorship of Schofield Thayer, was a key event. Thayer, with the aid of a group of intelligent young assistants, of whom Miss Moore was to be one, provided a firm and open-minded backing for informed discussion of every European and American artistic trend. For the first time in America, a magazine approaching the full intelligence and aesthetic dignity of certain European reviews was established. *The Dial* was the opposite of provincial: it published a series of "Letters" from European capitals, written not by journalists, but by creative writers. Its contributors were not forced into eccentricity by the nervousness of this editor or that; they were allowed leeway in which to gather themselves together and present their talents at leisure and at length. The ferments of the modern movement were given time and space in which to settle into patterns; and many of these patterns turned out to be fertile ones. Political theory here bore no weight; the aesthetic impulse was allowed to function without ideological compulsion. One of the most interesting phenomena of the twenties was the swiftness with which critical power developed, and the manner in which this criticism reinforced, and even kindled, creativeness. Because of the interplay between originality in writing and a criticism founded on fresh attitudes, a small but infinitely eager and educable audience for the arts in general was formed.

Moreover, the existence of *The Dial* brought out with ever-increasing clarity the fact of an obvious division between American *avant-garde* and American conventional writing. Poets were now regularly appearing on either side of an invisible formal line;

but differing attitudes toward form were becoming a
lesser consideration than truth of analysis and intensity of insight. To sing with charm, to assume the
traditional role of the bard, was no longer enough;
and displays of pure sophistication, it was becoming
clear, ran outside a deep and vital current which was
directing itself, with quiet but powerful force, toward
interpretation.

Nothing in the atmosphere of the beginning twenties pointed with direct promise toward the emergence of poetic vision; but a way for its emergence
had at least been cleared. In retrospect, it seems
right and fitting that the great poem of the era should
have appeared early and unexpectedly: *The Waste
Land,* published in *The Dial* in November 1922,
stands, in the first place, as a definition of boundary.
With it any possibility of further ignorance concerning the spiritual state of the modern world is closed.

The Waste Land was dedicated to Ezra Pound:
il migliore fabbro.[2] Eliot's sense of the disintegration—moral, spiritual and social—of European society had shown up, as we have seen, in his shorter
poems. A crisis in his own life and health brought
him, in the early twenties, to Switzerland. *The
Waste Land* opens with a description of an international invalid group, characteristic of sanitorium or
spa society. Eliot, from the poem's beginning, proves
himself the observer quick to catch and to organize
dramatically the dropped hints of disorganization and
despair expressed in the accents of contemporary
humanity, at all levels.

---

2. It has recently come to light that Pound acted as a critic and
editor upon the MS of *The Waste Land.* See Pound's *Letters* p.
169 ff.; see also Eliot's essay in *An Examination of Ezra Pound*
(Norfolk, Conn., *New Directions,* 1950), p. 28: "It was in 1922
that I placed before Pound in Paris the manuscript of a sprawling
chaotic poem called 'The Waste Land' which left his hands, reduced
to about half its size, in the form in which it appears in print."

The chief formal distinguishing feature of the long poem is its anthropological framework. Sir James Frazer's *The Golden Bough: A Study in Comparative Religions* had appeared in 1890; and at Cambridge University scholars headed by Gilbert Murray had for some years been engaged in applying anthropological findings to Greek literature. In 1920, Jessie Weston's *From Ritual to Romance* had explored the medieval Holy Grail legend by anthropological methods. Eliot makes acknowledgment to both Frazer and Weston. What Eliot came upon, says F. O. Matthiessen:

. . . was the recurring pattern in various myths, the basic resemblances, for example, between the vegetation myths of the re-birth of the year, the fertility myths of the re-birth of the potency of man, the Christian story of the Resurrection and the Grail legend of purification. The common source of all these . . . lay in the fundamental rhythm of nature—that of the death and re-birth of the year; and their varying symbolism was an effort to explain the origin of life. Such knowledge, along with the [recent] researches of psychology, pointed to the close union in all these myths of the physical and spiritual, to the fact that their symbolism was basically sexual . . . pointed, in brief, to the fundamental relation between the well-springs of sex and religion.

At the moment when Freud's discoveries in medical psychology and Frazer's in anthropology were beginning to filter into the popular consciousness— where they were to be turned to a variety of frivolous uses, when superficially applied—Eliot recognized them as possible carriers of a theme, and forged the first link between these important psychological and historical discoveries of his period and his period's poetry. So much concerning the modern human dilemma was brought into focus in *The Waste Land*, that new sources of energy and insight were released; the poem remains an almost inexhaustible reservoir of "vision" even after the passage of thirty years.

Far from being a poem of despair, it projects a picture of mankind at its highest point of ascetic control—St. Augustine, Buddha—as well as mankind at its lowest point of spiritual stupor, ignorance, and squalor. Moreover, *The Waste Land* opens out into timeless wisdom—"Give, Sympathize, Control"— and into a glimpse of that peace which passes understanding.

iv

Eliot's deep intuitive grasp of the postwar situation in Europe owed some of its strength to the detachment his American background afforded him. Many of the poetic talents which began to spring up in diverse quantity during the twenties shared this perspective only in part; while many were completely blank to it. The finest of these American talents, it is true, shared an impulse toward emotional veracity and intellectual analysis. Others were concerned merely with the more shallow motives of personal or stylistic revolt. Elements of unthinking obsession were evident in some, of fashionable exploitation in others. A crowd of imitators, opportunists, and *blageurs* helped to distort and confuse the picture.

Several main lines, however, are clear. One line followed an older poetic convention with some closeness: this was the line exemplified by the later Robinson and the later Frost. The Pulitzer prizes in poetry, from 1922, serve as a rather close guide to this conservative tendency. Robinson was given Pulitzer awards in 1922, 1925, and 1928; Frost was to receive these awards on four occasions: in 1924, 1931, 1937, and 1943. At the end of the twenties, a younger man was to pull the conservative line boldly over into the popular. This was Stephen Vincent Benét (1898-1943), who in 1929 won the Pulitzer Prize for his long poem *John Brown's Body* published the previous year: a poem which made use of (by then) thoroughly "bourgeoisified" folk patterns to color a sentimental historical narrative.

The Dial's awards favored experiment. They were given to Eliot in 1922, to Marianne Moore in 1921 and 1924; to E. E. Cummings in 1925, to William Carlos Williams in 1926, to Ezra Pound in 1927. The *Poetry* awards steered a fairly steady middle course, although with frequent surprising deviations toward both convention and innovation.

The tone of poetry began to range from serious to light with unself-conscious ease—a sign of vigor and of health. E. E. Cummings, a New Englander who had written a remarkable book, *The Enormous Room* (1922), concerning his experience as a prisoner in France, translated his recent acquaintance with French *avant-gardism,* "Dada," and the beginnings of surrealism into his own terms: the terms of an uncompromising Yankee wit with a youthful sense of the burlesque. *Tulips and Chimneys* (1923) was delightfully irreverent in form and fresh in feeling. Cummings' insistence, over a period of twenty-five years, on his youthful typographical oddities tended, as time went on, to become tiresome; and his failure to mature, emotionally and intellectually, finally introduced a note of peevishness into his work as a whole. The fact that he never swerved from a latent adolescent idealism, added to the fact of his permanent belief in certain simple (in the best sense) virtues, kept his work, for all its increasing bad temper and skittishness, basically serious and important.

Poetic groups came into being in certain regions up to this time rather parochially isolated from the main literary stream in America. The most impressive of these was the "Fugitive" group which centered around Vanderbilt University in Nashville, Tennessee. Here John Crowe Ransom, Allen Tate, Laura Riding Gottschalk, Elizabeth Madox Roberts and others formed a small nucleus of poetry and informed criticism that drew nourishment from certain Southern attitudes, from Eliot, and from contemporary French poetry—the work of Paul Valéry, for example. The importance of the introduction of this talented Southern opposition, into a scene where the emphasis had been largely upon the poetry produced by Easterners and Midwesterners, was undeniable; these writers soon made their talents felt in wider fields, without losing their idiosyncratic point of view. Later, the isolated Robinson Jeffers was to begin to construct a peculiar misanthropic world through a series of dramatic poems acted out against a wild background of California coastline. A New Orleans group, centering around the magaine *The Double Dealer* (1921-26), showed a certain amount of vitality and originality.

Throughout the twenties the "little magazine" was a powerful force, not only as a vehicle for creative writers, but as a forum where the conflicting aesthetic problems of the period could be explored and formulated. Many of these publications came out in France and Europe, following the footsteps of their restless editors, who were, without exception, young writers eager to absorb art and literature at their source. Thus, *Broom: An International Magazine of the Arts* (1921-24) was brought out in Rome, Berlin, and New York; *Laughing Horse* (1922-39) in California, Guadalajara, Sante Fé, and Taos; *Secession* (1922-24) in Vienna, Berlin, Florence, and New York. The most important "exile" of these little magazines was perhaps *The Transatlantic Review* published in Paris during a single year, from 1924 to 1925, and edited by Ford Madox Ford. The shortest lived was *Aesthete* (February 1925) which published one issue as a satirical reply to an attack upon aesthetes. Later in the decade, *transition,* with Eugene Jolas as editor, was to aid in developing "The Revolution of the Word" to its farthest limits, principally through its continued and reverent publication of James Joyce's "Work in Progress." Here the irrational elements in *avant-gardism* were raised to an extreme importance, and given an accompanying "philosophic" structure, largely based on the researches of psychoanalysis. *transition's* importance is now seen to be its introduction of European *avant-garde* writing on a wide scale, either in the original or in translation, as well as on its stubborn adherence to an extreme position, which was not without fruitful consequences.

v

In view of the confusion attendant upon the introduction and development, in the space of a few years, of such differing and explosive stylistic elements, it is remarkable that any reinforcement of the line of feeling was able to take place. This reinforcement was again chiefly due to a feminine vein of lyricism— a vein now reinvigorated by the addition of intellectual qualities. The work of Sara Teasdale (1884- 1933) had begun to free itself, in the twenties, from very nearly all traces of a romantic vocabulary and a romantic tone. The poems in *Flame and Shadow* (1920) are so naturally put together that they seem to be spoken, rather than written—spoken at the direct urging of passionate impulse. Miss Teasdale's lyrics, moreover, accompanied her experience of life step by step; they became increasingly lucid and tragic with the passage of time. She expressed not only the simplicities of traditional feminine feeling, but new subtleties of emotional nuance, and her last book, *Strange Victory,* published posthumously in 1933, shows classic depth and balance.

Even in an era of general revolt against moral conventions, a declaration of personal revolt is striking when uttered in a woman's voice. Edna St. Vincent Millay (1892-1950) took no part in the revolt against style. Her lyricism expressed itself in forms straight out of the Keatsian convention; and her modern mixture of abandonment and disillusion was almost always accompanied by classical ornament. At her best, she could cut into the center of complicated emotion with sharpness and unself-consciousness—a power which derived in part from her study of the Latin poets. At her worst, she fell victim to sentimentality and the dangers of self-pity and self-regard. Her New England background had in it sturdy elements upon which she could count, and she belonged to a generation filled with genuine feminist and liberal idealism. She formulated for a new generation of young women a standard of sexual defiance and "heroism" which, in spite of its romantic coloring, was marked by truth and pathos. A certain hampering nihilism, as well as a close attachment to literary fashion, apparent in Miss Millay from the outset, prevented her from breaking through to impressive maturity; but even her later work is filled with distinguished fragments. She often succeeded in transcending her worst faults. Many of her sonnets are in the great tradition; and that she was, by nature, a lyric poet of the first order, is an incontestable fact.

The gifts of Elinor Wylie (1885-1928) brought to the feminine lyric a mature emotional richness, as well as an added brilliance of craftsmanship. Mrs. Wylie early caught the note of Eliot's shorter poems.

Nets to Catch the Wind (1921) revealed, as well, a first-hand apprenticeship to Donne, Herbert, and Marvell. For a time she seemed overwhelmed by her own virtuosity; but she became more tellingly controlled as time went on, and in her last volume achieved a power that was directly structural. Although an undertone of rather inflated romanticism was constantly in evidence, her work as a whole was far more complex than that of any feminine predecessor.

A younger woman, Léonie Adams (1899-   ) in these same years was able completely to escape from the atmosphere of modishness that clung in some degree to the work of Miss Millay and Mrs. Wylie. Her first volume *Those Not Elect* (1925) was again written in form—in stanzas lightly touched by Elizabethan, rather than by metaphysical, lyricism. By means of this coloring, Miss Adams' sensitively interpreted nature, thought, and feeling have an intensity which often seem to slip over into mystic vision.

The period's growing appreciation of the implicit is evident in the enthusiasm accorded the revived work of Emily Dickinson. In 1924, Mme Martha Dickinson Bianchi, Miss Dickinson's niece, brought out what she then described as the *Complete Poems,* along with a volume of *Life and Letters;* at the same time Conrad Aiken introduced a volume of *Selected Poems* to English readers. The homage now tendered the Amherst recluse was warmer than any she had previously received. She was recognized as the possessor of a poetic vision at times as penetrating as Blake's. The oddities of her style, her "off rhymes," and her instinctive sense of compression had now become acceptable; and the romantic legend which soon began to fasten itself to the facts of her life, as well as the devotion of a large public to the more childish "Emily," could not obscure the pure radiance of the mature poet Dickinson.

In 1925, Paul Rosenfeld, a young "impressionist" critic, who, like Huneker before him (although with more intellectual equipment than his forerunner) took all the arts for his province, was able to state in *Port of New York* that America had become a good place in which to live "due to the labor of a dozen artists' hands." Another critic remarked a few years later that "Americans for the first time in their history are seeking honest self-knowledge instead of self-glorification. . . . [The nation] is [now] willing to be told the bitter truth, so long as it is told something about itself." In the field of poetry, as in the field of literature in general, not a dozen hands, but hundreds, had made contribution. If the end of the twenties seemed to be signalized by a complete and disastrous deflation of inflated aesthetics, as well as of overextended economics, a total retreat back to unenlightened and naïve values could not, and did not, come to pass. The development of schools and styles, the revolts against inner and outer pressures which, in Europe, had taken place over a long period of time, in England and America had proceeded, in a single ten years, at perhaps too rapid a pace. A period of relative creative quiet had to follow upon such abundance and confusion. The decade of the thirties, in spite of its entanglements with barren Marxian theory, was to be a time when American poetry—and poetry in English in general—would be deepened and enriched by influences hitherto ignored; a time when the false would be gradually sifted out from the genuine; a time when publics would be surely defined; a time of comparisons and reconciliations.

VIII

IDEOLOGY AND IRRATIONALISM,
1930-1941

IT IS USUAL to think of poetry in America in the
1930's as overwhelmingly influenced by Marxist ideology. The decade, as a matter of fact, was one in
which a variety of influences made striking impact
upon the poetic situation, so that even Marxian pressures, so strong at the beginning, were split and
altered as the ten years advanced. It is important,
however, to fix our attention at first upon the way in
which Marxist theory came to affect poetic careers.

American artists, writers, and intellectuals had
been more or less open and sympathetic to radical
ideas since the success of the Leninist revolution in
1917. A rather romantic interest in the Russian
proletarian "success" was a factor in the general
breaking of codes, in the early twenties. Magazines
with an avowed radical political background had
been generous in publishing young poets and illus-
trators, from the days of the founding of *The Masses*
(1911). Bohemianism and socialism were a natural
mixture, in the early days of civic reform, feminism,
and an awakening labor movement. The wartime
suppression of *The Seven Arts* and of *The Masses*
(1917) and the trial of *The Masses'* editors (1918)
provided rallying points for a "liberal" protest in
which many writers took part. *The Liberator*, which
supplanted *The Masses* in 1918, published poetry,
experimental and otherwise, the revolutionary flavor
of which was often mild or nonexistent.

The Wall Street crash of 1929 not only seriously
damaged the functioning of American finance-cap-

italism, but also set boundaries to the American dream of unlimited success within a capitalist framework. This crisis provided organized Marxist forces with new fields into which their propaganda could be extended—the field of the middle class and the field of the artist. Established left-wing authority immediately began to marshal directives and frame rules aimed at the conversion of members of these groups to Marxian beliefs. In an atmosphere of actual want and prevailing fear these methods began to take hold, often in the case of men and women whose aesthetic position had formerly been unshakeable. Many individuals, temperamentally complex and seemingly intellectually balanced, embraced the simple and rigid patterns of the Marxist faith with mixed feelings of exhaustion and relief. It is important to remember that many of these converts came to Marxism with the highest of humane motives, although the neurotic motives of others were only too apparent.

The first important talent in America to be drawn into a close relationship with the operation of idealistic materialism was that of Hart Crane (1899-1932). Crane's suicide at the age of 32 occurred when the decade's more rigorous formulations of Marxian theory and practice had just begun. Crane's poetry at no point reflects Marxian dogma. But Crane's efforts to absorb and acclimatize the machine into poetry and to distill symbolic values from the facts of an urban and mechanized civilization, as well as his underlying Whitmanian optimism concerning the linked destinies of man and machine, appealed strongly to the liberals of his period, and gave him an attentive and admiring audience among them. Crane himself was far more attracted by the mysteries of Einsteinian physics, the clue thrown up by Whitehead's philosophy, and even by Ouspensky's theory of "cosmic consciousness" than by the details of the class struggle. *The Bridge* published in 1930, was his major attempt to create an essentially religious myth from the facts of modern man's soaring technical triumphs; to relate these technical feats to a vast universal design. This myth was originally intended to be loaded with hope for the future. Man's will had produced artifacts which could be taken as visible and material bonds between the seen and the unseen; these had within them life-giving elements, and the poet could tremble on the verge of worship when faced with them. ·

Crane's symbol broke down not merely because Crane's vision was inadequate, but because his faith in his precarious imaginative connections was never steady. Despair and the facts of evil kept breaking into his pure design. He himself could not help but realize that his wish to construct extenuating spiritual faith from physical facts was mistaken from the first; and his knowledge of his initial mistake keeps breaking through, in flashes of poetic insight. Crane tried consciously to enlarge and extend his moments of vision, but the result was too often delirium rather than further clarity. His style was at moments a controlled one, in the emerging modern manner; at other times it tended to become inflated with romantic rhetoric.

Crane mistook Eliot's penetrating analysis of modern spiritual ills for cyncism and despair, and tried to counter an attitude which he thought false by an apocalyptic faith which he had moments of thinking complete. The truth, soon to be recognized by poets who closely followed him in time, that the more man is mechanized, the more he is alone, was a truth that Crane sensed intuitively; it is upon his unconscious knowledge of this truth that his best work is based. In spite of the thrilling beauty of many isolated lines in *The Bridge* and the very nearly realized statement of his imaginative theme in its *Proem,* Crane's real successes lie in his short lyrics, especially in those which deal with primitive and tropical surroundings. The poems based on his experience of Caribbean islands, which display a wealth of natural detail against the ever-present background of a tragically realized tropic sea, show how exquisitely the ardor of Crane's temperament could express itself when provided with sympathetic material.

For Crane, in spite of his moods of depression, was a poet of acceptance and of celebration, not a creature of fear or despair. His temperament was fundamentally sanguine. He never fully explored his anguish, and he was unable to pass over into a full passionate rejection like Rimbaud, to whom he is often mistakenly compared. When he at length discovered that his power of a perennial return to joy was blocked, he cut short the process of living. He died at the beginning of a transitional decade in which, on the one hand, guilt and cruelty were to be released and used toward preconceived ends; while, on the other, all spiritual compromise was to be proved vain, and all ecstatic celebration of baseless and premature hope was to be defeated. His reputation, seen in perspective, is secure. In spite of troubled times and his own disordered nature, the compass of his genius never deviated widely from true imaginative north.

ii

Before we examine the poetry written in the thirties which was based on Marxist conviction, it is

important to mention the non-Marxian elements released into the creative stream of the times, since
many of these endured after Marxian piety had
faded. Eliot's *Ash Wednesday* (1930) announced
not only the beginning of his Christian faith, but a
change of style; here the last of his youthful bitterness merges with the intimations of a new pathos
and a new humility. The second edition of Gerard
Manley Hopkins's *Poems,* published in the same year,
under Charles Williams' sympathetic editorship, enlarged the Hopkins revival which had been initiated
by the first edition, edited by Robert Bridges in 1918.
It was now made clear that the work of this English
Jesuit scholar belonged to the great tradition of English poetry. It was also made clear that Hopkins, a
Catholic convert who in the sixties of the preceding
century had been one of Jowett's "bright young men"
at Balliol, was closely allied with, if not superior to,
the baroque poets of the seventeenth century. He
was a mystic in their grand manner, with an added
modern intensity and realism. His style was quickly
taken up by imitators, but, as Charles Williams truly
remarks, "Hopkins was not the child of vocabulary
but of passion." It is finally impossible to capture
and reproduce a style whose original impetus came
from a ceaseless and finally unresolved struggle between conflicting spiritual and moral forces. Hopkins'
experiments with sprung rhythm—a metric system
which may be loosely described as fairly even in
count of stress, but extremely free in count of
syllables—was soon widely imitated, and marks of
his compression, ellipses and deletions are today
commonly observable in poetic usage.

At the same time, in Ireland, Yeats was writing in
the full idiomatic ease of his later style, as well as
in the widened angle of his later vision of men and

events. A collection, *The Tower,* published in 1928, was followed by *The Winding Stair* (1933). Pound secluded since 1925 in Rapallo, was at work on his *Cantos,* the first of which, "A Draft of XVI Cantos for the Beginning of a Poem of Some Length," had been printed in 1925 in Paris. Pound's retirement was comparative only; his recently published *Letters* show that his drive toward the discovery and subsequent organization of "originality" had by no means lessened. His creative forces, however, were being more and more channeled in the direction of a personal dogma. The *Cantos,* begun as a fantasia on classical, Dantesque, Renaissance, and modern themes, soon became caught in the gears of Pound's growing obsession with the fact and the power of money. A shrillness of tone as well as a scattering of ideas had become evident as early as 1933, when "A Draft of XXX Cantos" was published in England and America. However, a fragmentary sense of design and an unfailing power of language remained and reacted with positive force on the poetry of certain contemporaries.

It must be remembered, as well, that, although periodicals like *The Dial* and *transition* had succumbed to depressed economic conditions, direct access by the American public to certain large key works of modern prose was now possible. The last volume of Proust's *A la recherche du temps perdu* had been translated into English in 1928, under the title *The Past Recaptured.* The American ban upon Joyce's *Ulysses* (1922) had been lifted in 1933. Thomas Mann's *Der Zauberberg,* first published in 1924, had also been translated, and its thought and symbolism made available to American readers. Meanwhile, the scattered critical insights of the twenties were being examined and arranged by

Americans and Englishmen. Edmund Wilson's *Axel's Castle* (1931) related twentieth-century poetic style to nineteenth-century French origins. I. A. Richards described in *Practical Criticism* (1929) the results of his "scientific" teaching in the poetic field at Cambridge University. His pupil, William Empson, subjected poetic subtlety to analysis at many levels of meaning in *Seven Types of Ambiguity* (1931). In all these works, whether imaginative or critical, the complex and evasive spirit of modernity was weighed and examined; and the critical works brought the sharpest sort of rational analytic method to bear on the poetic expression of the symbolic and the irrational.

Meanwhile, a school of poetry devoted to the exploitation of the irrational, whenever found (in the subconscious, in manifestations of insanity, in the mentality of savages and children), was gaining adherents in France, England, and Europe in general. This was the surrealist school under the leadership of André Breton. Breton had been active in the postwar Dada movement which had come from Switzerland to Paris in 1919. Tristan Tzara and his followers, even before the war, had set out "to organize an enormous mystification" as an indictment of respectable European institutions. In the midst of the shock and disillusionment brought on by the war's end, "Dada," a term which meant nothing, was no longer considered so much "a wrecking enterprise" (for everything had been torn down) as "an inventory of the ruins, and a declaration of the failure and death of a civilization." This attitude of total negation was soon transformed, however, into a more positive program and creed. Breton, a born organizer much on the order of Pound, began, in

1924, to issue a series of surrealist "manifestos."
Breton outlined a belief in the power of the marvelous: "the marvelous alone is beautiful." Mankind
could only be saved "by a wave of dream;" the individual subconscious was the one source of power.
This power, if released and manipulated, could trans-
form the world.

Surrealism, by 1930, had already split into "tran-
scendent" and political groups. Breton countered the
desertion of some of his followers by the expulsion
of others; and surrealism, although continuing to
operate effectively in the field of the graphic arts, began to dwindle, in the field of literature. Breton and
his faithful follower Paul Eluard were for a time the
only poets of any consequence in nonpolitical surrealism, but reinforcements soon appeared from Central Europe, in the mass emigration of *avant-garde*
writers after the setting up of Hitler's regime. After
1936 literary surrealism gained power not only in
France but in England and America. Traces of
Eluard's rather delicate and lyrical methods are
recognizable from this point on in the work of American and English *avant-gardists;* Breton's rhetoric—
which often echoes Victor Hugo at his most formidable—later became noticeable, not only among
young experimentalists during the forties, but in the
work of older and more established poets.

iii

The first strikingly original and well-written "Marxist" poetry to attract attention in the early thirties,
was published in England—the work of three young
men who had been friends at Oxford: W. H. Auden,
Stephen Spender, and C. Day Lewis. These young
men, born in the first decade of this century, had
grown up in an England of postwar unemployment

and the dole, of abandoned pit-heads in depressed mining areas, during the years of an Empire's declining power. For them, "the slump" represented only an intensification of conditions they had observed from childhood; they were unable to observe or describe their environment without taking into truthful account its enveloping atmosphere of breakdown, waste, and disintegration. The attitude of young Americans toward depression conditions was not so broadly based; the young Englishmen were working from facts long present in their daily lives, rather than from an experience of sudden shock. Their poems, therefore, could be expressed in a variety of emotional tones and by a range of stylistic devices; they were not limited to shrill cries of despair, a series of grim marching orders, or to turgid and humorless projections of fear and guilt.

Auden, from the beginning (his first volume, *Poems,* appeared in 1930) gave evidence of large gifts. He combined depth of insight with brilliance of method. With young authority he took over several styles, and fused them into something quite original and quite his own. From Dadaism and the early surrealism of Jarry and Apollinaire he had learned the effective use of parody and lampoon; his use of Anglo-Saxon compression stemmed from Pound's early "The Seafarer" and from Hopkins; he also took up and elaborated certain popular styles, from music-hall patter songs to negro "blues." He had learned lightness from the nonsense verse of Lear and Carroll, and from Gilbert's librettos, as well as tricks of assonance from Wilfred Owen. The prevailing tone of his earliest poetry combined sharp satire with an appraising and sensitive tenderness; and he soon developed a remarkable flexibility of approach which allowed him to turn a subject, for the reader's attention, completely into view, by means of attacking it from various angles.

Both Auden and Spender spent some time in pre-Hitler Germany; and there came into contact not only with the work of the modern Austrian writers, Rilke and von Hofmannsthal, but with a revived interest in the eighteenth-century Hölderlin. Hölderlin's pure classicism was countered, in the Germany of the time, by the direct adherence to the Marxist revolutionary doctrine of the poet-dramatist Berthold Brecht. Brecht's hatred and suspicion of "bourgeois servility and deceit" expressed itself in poetry openly opposed to bourgeois "elegance, nobility and charm." Auden's early poetry, reflecting the opposition of these influences, gained tension thereby.

Spender's poems were more unbrokenly romantic; but he could accommodate his method to remarkable evocations of modern energy, color, and speed. C. Day Lewis, writing with a conventional crispness and less interest in stylistic experiment, showed at the beginning a closer devotion to Marxian ideology than either of his colleagues, whose chief interest was "to warn," and to promulgate a feeling of suspense before impending disaster. To these English talents, the Anglo-Irish gifts of another young Oxonian was soon joined. Louis MacNeice's *Poems* (1935) exhibited a poetic equipment almost as dazzling as Auden's stemming from a Celtic delight in the play of language and of wit.

The work of Auden and Spender, and of Lewis and MacNeice, published in America in 1934 and thereafter, immediately attracted admirers and imitators. The prevailing tone of American leftist poetry, however, was not at once noticeably lightened or diversified. It continued to be confused in statement, and emotionally numb. While the imagination of Auden darted about, illuminating with bitter gaiety one aspect of contemporary life after another; while Spender often intensified his picture of the human dilemma with melancholy splendor of language; while Lewis, in neat and telling stanzas, invented effective symbols for social and political bafflement, and MacNeice sang of contemporary crises and follies to a bagpipe air, American poets settled down to an almost unbroken level of gloomy conviction and gloomier hope. Moreover, a good many dark shadows of an undefeated Puritanism again became visible and menacing.

Range of interest, power of imagination, and a certain originality appeared in the work of Muriel Rukeyser (1913-) and Kenneth Fearing (1902-). Miss Rukeyser, in her *Theory of Flight* (1935) and *U. S. 1* (1938) endeavored to express her sense of righteous indignation by means of a series of symbolic frames closely allied to reality. Her style, an amalgam of modern styles, was almost wholly unrelieved by moments of clarity, or her seriousness by moments of lightness. As a result her argument was not able to project itself with force, and her long poems failed in impact, because of dramatic as well as structural incoherence. Kenneth Fearing approached his problems with the aid of an irony sometimes reminiscent of the early Masters. He dramatized his material with effect in short poems whose wisecracking surface smoothness served to point up and intensify the ugly facts with which he dealt. Fearing's *Angel Arms* (1929) and *Poems* (1935) display vigor and direction.

The most dramatic and unexpected conversion to

a political point of view occurred in the case of Archibald MacLeish (1892-   ). Mr. MacLeish, whose first books belonged to the aesthetic of the twenties, originally was a defender of that aesthetic. He followed closely in the footsteps of those American poets who drew refreshment from the French; and later went directly to French *avant-gardists* such as Apollinaire, for mood as well as matter. His elaboration and dilution of these sources was particularly apparent in *Conquistador* (1932), a long poem based on Bernal Diaz del Castillo's account (1632) of the Spanish conquest of Mexico. Here MacLeish manipulated Pound's methods, Eliot's tone, St. John Perse's vocabulary, as well as Hopkin's compression and Wilfred Owen's assonance—with astounding ease. The final effect, however, in spite of minor brilliances, was that of pastiche. That such pastiche was acceptable to many readers was proved, not only by the book's comparative popularity, but by the fact that it won a Pulitzer prize in 1933.

MacLeish at first took a firm stand against poetry as propaganda. He advanced into his political stand slowly; the volume *Public Speech* (1936) finally announced his political and social convictions. He continued to express these convictions—through the media of radio playwriting and collaboration in writing film scripts, as well as through his poetry— up to and beyond the outbreak of war in 1941. So firm and ardent was his belief in the worth of "social justice" that he came to the point of accusing those writers who had held to purely aesthetic motives as breakers of morale, under the disapprobating title "The Irresponsibles." This sort of blame was indicative, as has been said, of a latent Puritanism in the American ethos which has never been completely resolved, as well as of a manifestation of acute patriotism in time of crisis. For a short period, middle-class hostilities to art became open and general, but, happily, this hostility lessened, or at least became less vocal, as the war period ended.

IX

POETRY AT THE HALF-CENTURY,
1939-1950

IT IS THROUGH the acceptance of a variety of aesthetic and intellectual points of view that a culture is given breadth and density. Without such acceptance, rooted in a sincere liberality and tolerance of spirit, any cultural situation is bound to become one-sided and impoverished. The American arts in general, from the end of the thirties to the present day, notwithstanding the interruption of the war years, have steadily been enriched by their absorption of differing standards and talents, both native and foreign. This absorption is still going on, although at a slightly slower rate than formerly.

A general sifting out and rearrangement of values has accompanied this accumulation of artistic substance. And a diversified critical approach, by providing fruitful points of argument, has helped bring general attention to poets and critics of the past whose work has bearing on the present. These exemplars, very often, are new choices; even the hierarchy of French nineteenth-century writing has been altered, rearranged and simplified. The symbolist movement is now seen to start with Baudelaire; and Valéry plainly continues and develops Mallarméan principles. Certain prose writers have come to be recognized as poetic "references": André Gide and Henry James now stand in this relation.

A good many false reputations have disappeared or been eliminated, while the work of certain writers, previously fallen into neglect or disrepute, has been restored to a dignified status. Oscar Wilde has thus been given a certain dignity; and from a more remote past, so has the poetry of Melville, Beddoes, Christopher Smart, and John Clare.

A remarkable number of translations were published in America, from the early thirties on. An almost exclusive interest in modern French literature was broken by the emergence of two powerful European talents: that of Federico García Lorca (1899-1936) and of Rainer Maria Rilke (1875-1926). García Lorca, an Andalusian poet and playwright, had been attracted to the folk song of his region, which, like the folk song of Yeats's Ireland, had remained living and intact in a country where industrialization came late. García Lorca wrote a series of early ballads and songs wherein a modern expressionist brilliance is employed to accent the poignance of native Spanish and gypsy themes. He lived for a short time in New York and Cuba (1929-30); his American experience coincided with a surrealist phase, and lead into a new interest in urban negro life and music. On his return to Spain, he was active in the Spanish theater. Translations of his work include *Poems* (1939) by Stephen Spender and J. L. Gili and *The Poet in New York* (1940) by Rolfe Humphries. García Lorca was shot by a fascist firing squad in his native city of Granada in 1936, although his connection with Spanish politics had been very nearly non-existent. His work added rhythm, color, and human warmth to experimentalism—up to that time rather cold in tone and monotonous in form; and was widely imitated.

This Spaniard's poetry, so dramatically connected with the trouble and violence of his time, burst into sudden prominence. Rilke's poetry, on a larger scale and of a greater depth than García Lorca's, came to the notice of English and American readers more gradually. Rilke's own life had been composed of a series of steps toward serenity and self-knowledge, many of them wavering and tentative. Born in Prague, under the old Austrian regime, and throughout his life a restless wanderer throughout Europe, Rilke from the first considered himself a "dedicated" poet. Paris came to be his center of activity, and he was for a time Rodin's secretary. That Rilke never developed a sense of responsibility toward others and lived for long periods upon what remained of noble patronage in pre-1914 Europe, are facts that have been used against him by his detractors. The final triumph of his later poetry, produced in loneliness and self-exile in Switzerland at the end of his life and career, is proof that his self-absorption was justified. His *Duinesen Elegien* and *Sonette an Orpheus,* written at Muzot in the canton of Valais, have been called "the most impressive sequence of great poetry in modern European literature."

A translation of Rilke's chief prose work was published in America in 1930, under the title *The Journal of My Other Self.* It received little notice. An inadequate translation of scattered lyrics had appeared as early as 1918. British interest in Rilke really began with the translation and publication of his works in London. His true poetic quality was thus indicated in the translation (1931) of the *Elegien* by Victoria and Edward Sackville-West, and of shorter poems translated by J. B. Leishman, remarkable in their fidelity to the originals. American interest was soon stimulated by the translations of M. D. Herder Norton, which began to appear in 1934. Stephen Spender and Leishman collaborated in a rendering of the *Elegien* in 1939, under the title *Duino Elegies;* C. F. MacIntyre brought out *Fifty*

Selected Poems in 1940; and Mrs. Norton *Sonnets to Orpheus* in 1942. Many other English versions of Rilke's letters and poems followed.

Rilke's entire life can be regarded as a quest for certitude of a religious kind, although he rejected the appeal of orthodox Christianity, just as he rejected that of psychoanalysis. His early religiosity was shaped by his early sentimentality; but from 1907 on, his was undoubtedly the role of "a seeker." The final poems—ecstatic affirmations of faith and of joy—are unique in their power of inclusion as well as in their power of transcendence. However secular they may seem, and closely meshed with the figures of pagan antiquity as they are, there is no doubt that they are cries of the spirit, and of a modern spirit, that has at last found a way beyond the anxieties and the despair latent in contemporary reality. The enthusiasm with which these poems were received, in a decade when the tenets of dialectical materialism were widely accepted, was a proof that all traces of spiritual interest had not been erased from the modern consciousness.

Rilke's "passionate attempt to penetrate to the core of life itself" was one of many desperate attempts to reach beyond the grim standards of a secularized world, made by European intellectuals and artists, during the first part of the century. In France, certain spectacular conversions to the Catholic faith had stemmed from the prevailing sense of spiritual bafflement, felt by sensitive natures, in the midst of materialist successes of all kinds, on all levels of life and thought. The emphasis upon spiritual regeneration, so marked in the later poetry of Eliot and in Auden's middle phase, was accompanied by an openly expressed adherence to an orthodox religious faith, Anglo-Catholicism, on the part of both men. Eliot's poetry, from *Ash Wednesday* (1930) on, became increasingly religious in implication as well as increasingly dramatic in form. Eliot stated his belief in the social function of the drama in his lectures *The Use of Poetry and the Use of Criticism* (1933):

> The most useful poetry, socially, would be one which could cut across all the present stratifications of public taste. . . . The ideal medium for poetry, to my mind, and the most direct means of "social usefulness" for poetry is the theatre.

Sweeney Agonistes: Fragments of an Aristophanic Melodrama (1932), written in nervous and heavily accented rhythms that recalled the music hall, was Eliot's first, and unfinished, dramatic experiment. Eliot here explored, in a stylized manner which was never to be wholly absent from his later dramatic writing, the monotony and emptiness, the violence, fear, and guilt of lives lived upon the instinctual level, by means of a kind of nightmare caricature. His subsequent involvement in the writing of "a book of words" for the religious pageant *The Rock* (1934) resulted in some fine individual choruses. *Murder in the Cathedral* (1935), his first complete play, still retains, as a recent critic has pointed out, elements of the pageant and the ballet. Eliot as dramatist put into practice many of the formal procedures he admires in late Elizabethan drama. From Jonson he has taken over a certain broadness in dealing with character; and his central dramatic effects, it has been pointed out, depend upon classic structure—a contrast between the Hero and the Chorus.[1] It is interrelation of character with theme that gives his dramatic work subtlety; it is from his reiteration of

----

1. See M. C. Bradbrook's *T. S. Eliot* (British Council and Longmans, London, 1950.)

the importance of "the moment of choice" that his later plays, *The Family Reunion* (1939) and *The Cocktail Party* (1950), receive their religious relevance.

Eliot's shorter poems of the thirties express a new calm and a new pathos. "Marina" is perhaps the central poem of this group; a resolved conflict passes over into new life and new hope. In the "Corialan" poems the poet "warns." Here is the world of the dictator and the frustrated statesman: new power pitted against obsolete strategy, with the helpless crowd trapped between.

Auden's turn toward a spiritual resolution was announced by the poems, chiefly sonnets, he contributed to *Journey to a War* (1939), written in collaboration with Christopher Isherwood. Auden's attachment to left-wing ideology had become increasingly tenuous. His early plays, also written with Isherwood, *The Dog Beneath the Skin* (1935) and *The Ascent of F-6* (1936), were satires concerned with the general invalidism of bourgeois society in all its aspects. His belief in the efficacy of "the class war," as a cure of these ills, was not total; he realized from the beginning their psychic source. His nature, at once adventuresome and generous, needed a faith more humane than that of Marxism. Once this faith was found, Auden's genius began to function with a new freedom within bounds. His later work, *Another Time* (1940), *The Double Man* (1941), and *For the Time Being* (1944), increasingly deepens, without losing any of its brilliance or variety. He begins to strike notes of tenderness as well as of wit; he is able to range between the heights of oratory and the simplicities of the song. Auden came to America in 1938 and became a citizen in 1946. In *The Age of Anxiety* (1947) he takes the New York

scene as a background for a scathing analysis of contemporary character. This *Baroque Ecologue* with
its extraordinary virtuosity of style and its penetrating conclusions, won the Pulitzer Prize in 1948.

Side by side with the orthodox faith of Eliot and
Auden, the climate of American poetry was now so
tempered that it could not only produce but sustain
the moralistic and tightly formal poetry of Yvor
Winters and his California school; the aesthetic
"philosophy" of Wallace Stevens; the poetic socio-
logical investigations of William Carlos Williams in
Paterson: Books I-IV (1946-50); the "observations"
of Marianne Moore; the "reactionary" poetry of
Tate, and the sophisticated Southern balladry of
Ransom and Robert Penn Warren; as well as the
romantic idealism of Cummings. American poetry
had attained civilized breadth, without losing, in any
appreciative degree, its vital essence.

ii

By the middle forties a modern poetic style in
English had come into being, broadly workable and
capable of a variety of applications. This style was
a composite one, derived from many sources. But,
since very nearly all of the sources were genuine, the
end product was itself authentic. It was a style which
tended to veer, it is true, toward verbalism on the
one hand, and extreme condensation of meaning and
idea, on the other. At its worst, a core of overcom-
pressed thought was surrounded by an envelope of
overinflated words. It was a style rich in allusion,
and its tone could vary from conversational flatness
to high incantation. Its best practitioners, old and
young, had insight into the nature and possibilities
of their poetic means, and kept these flexible, according to the nature of the poetic end in view.

Young poets of the period had before them the example of still active older talents. Yeats died in 1939, but he had continued to be a provocative influence into extreme old age. Pound's *Cantos,* up to the late thirties, w h e n they became thoroughly warped in idea and overvehement in expression, were sources of one kind of originality. The influence of Auden was for a time not only pervasive but overpowering; but later his intricacy both of thought and expression, made him progressively less open to imitation. Although Breton had come to America during the war and had issued a third surrealist manifesto in New York in 1942, and although French surrealism was widely translated, surrealist influence was seldom directly apparent. Its effects, however, were widely diffused in the work of young experimentalists, from 1936 on. But surrealism's violent exploitation of the subconscious had led nowhere, and surrealist claims tended to evaporate into nonsense, as time went on.

The later work of Marianne Moore, Wallace Stevens, and William Carlos Williams became centers of emulation. Stevens, who had been almost totally silent after the publication of his first volume, *Harmonium* (1923), began to produce in quantity soon after the book's reissue in a revised form (1931). *Ideas of Order* and *Owl's Clover* appeared in limited editions in 1935 and 1936. Stevens's reputation had grown, rather than diminished, during his absence from the poetic scene, and *The Man With a Blue Guitar* (1937) found a small but appreciative audience. Stevens now had a theme—that of the importance of the imagination—and the tensions between the world of reality and the world of creative illusion became his constant preoccupation. Stevens's later poetry permits personal emotion to appear only obliquely; but such emotion continually invades his later work, almost, it would seem, without his knowledge.

Marianne Moore's later poetry, from the publication of *What Are Years?* (1941) and *Nevertheless* (1944), became warmer and more direct. Without losing any of her delightful innocence of approach, she no longer circled about human problems, but touched them at their heart, and openly praised life for its powers of transcendence and endurance, as well as for its astonishing multiplicity of form. Her poetry continued, as Eliot remarks, in the Preface to her *Selected Poems* (1935), "[to] form part of the body of durable poetry written in our time—in which an original sensibility and an alert intelligence and deep feeling have been engaged in maintaining the life of the English language."

William Carlos Williams's insistence on the importance of American speech rhythms and of a continual effort on the part of American poets to seek out the essential meaning of their surroundings, was a refreshing reminder to the young that the stuff of art is frequently crude and constantly available.

This reminder had pertinence, for, in contrast to the richness and variety of the creative gifts which exploded into being after 1912, a later generation, though generally far more informed and better equipped than their elders, found themselves functioning in a period of absorption, rather than in one of energetic projection. Such pauses are usual in any cultural progression; and they are marked by a diminution of creative vitality. A stiffening of method becomes evident; a drying out of emotion takes place. A growth of self-consciousness points to a return of skepticism and relative timidity.

At present, this tendency toward expertness and

control—toward conscious manipulation of texture, conscious heightening of tension, and conscious distillation of meaning—is accompanied by what seems to be a complete exhaustion of experimentalism. This exhaustion again follows a natural sequence. There are limits, as Eliot has recently pointed out, to "[an] extreme awareness and concern for language . . . [it is] something which must ultimately break down, owing to an increasing strain against which the human mind and nerves will rebel." Means alone cannot become the sole preoccupation of any art; their extreme refinement leads toward brittleness and fragility, while their extreme elaboration is in effect both enervating and stultifying. Modern poets, as had been said, now have at hand technical means of the utmost variety. But a generation of experimentalists has not worked with the sole aim of providing their successors with efficient tools. A knowledge of the uses to which these tools must be put, and of the regions to which they must penetrate, is of first importance.

It is the timber of poetry that wears most surely, and there is no timber that has not strong roots among the clay and worms. . . . Even if we grant that exalted poetry can be kept successful by itself, the strong things of life are needed in poetry also, to show that what is exalted or tender is not made by feeble blood. It may almost be said that before verse can be human again it must learn to be brutal.

This is John Millington Synge speaking in 1908; poetry was forced to learn the lesson indicated thereafter. And whenever new poetic force asserts itself, we can be sure that it will be accompanied by a new insight into the importance of Synge's remark.

iii

Numerous young poets emerged during the forties. The works of some were brought on prematurely by the war; some still clung to Marxist dogma; others were pure experimentalists. Some, moreover, were pedants; others merely learned and ambitious young men who had decided that the writing of poetry gave them prestige, academic or otherwise. Very nearly all the members of this poetic generation functioned, to a greater or less degree, within the pervasive influence of the composite modern style—a style which was steadily returning, by degrees, to "form." This style often served to cloak poverty of thought and immaturity of feeling. Thus, certain poets, by manipulating surfaces with skill, seemed more gifted than they actually were: they proved to be more fixated at childish emotional levels than a superficial examination of their writing had seemed to indicate.

Randall Jarrell (1914-   ), born in Tennessee and educated at Vanderbilt University, began his career as a witty and acute critic of poetry. His first book of poems, *Blood for a Stranger* (1942), showed cleverness rather than originality. His second volume, *Little Friend, Little Friend* (1945), in which his war experience came into view, dealt with complicated as well as with brutally simplified situations with direct though bitter sympathy. The poetry of Delmore Schwartz (1913-   ), openly derives literature from literature. Schwartz displayed the full range of modern stylistic effects, and the full apparatus of modern emotional attitudes, with a certain saving amount of naïveté. Every trick of style, every favored subject was now out in the open; later poets would avoid these clichés with more care.

Karl Shapiro (1913-   ) was able to get through to the commonplace. He combined, in his early poems, insight with subtlety, and made himself a master of the dramatic lyric. He produced one of the few war poems worth reading—written, it goes with-

out saying, in the form of an elegy. Elizabeth Bishop
(1911-   ), in spite of her reverence for Miss
Moore, had her own material and tone, which she
continued to develop. Robert Lowell (1917-   ),
a descendant of New England Calvinists, after his
conversion to Roman Catholicism evolved a massive
lyric-dramatic talent close to the baroque. Tech-
nically elaborate and weighted with tragic feeling,
the poems in *Land of Unlikeness* (1944) and *Lord
Weary's Castle* (1946) have moments of true gran-
deur. A distinct improvement in the Pulitzer Prize
committee's standards of value is proved by the fact
that Shapiro and Lowell, as well as W. H. Auden,
were given Pulitzer awards.

Peter Viereck (1916-   ), a versatile satirist,
began to re-examine those areas of modernism which
had become sterile, and to subject certain contemporary literary and moral pretensions to mockery: a
healthful sign in years when major battles long since
won kept reappearing in slightly altered minor forms.
Richard Wilbur (1921-   ), the youngest of this
group, has proved himself in two books, *The Beautiful Changes* (1947) and *Ceremony* (1950), a subtle
lyricist of the first order. Behind these signal figures
a number of talents very nearly equal in sensitiveness
existed: the work of Richard Eberhart, Theodore
Roethke, and others gave variety and depth to the
picture.

iv

The story of American poetry as it developed
during the first fifty years of the twentieth century
should not conclude with a naming of young names,
or an examination of incomplete careers. The final
emphasis should fall on the large, conclusive, and
central facts of the period's achievement; and that
achievement should be related to the development of

other arts, and of American "culture" in general. The student of the subject can fruitfully engage himself in making such relations if certain broad outlines are made clear.

At a first retrospective glance, the true triumph in every modern art appears to be that of sincerity over sham, of naturalness over affectation, of a striking turn toward precision, analysis, and structure; of a wider range of conception and idea; of a deeper apprehension of meaning. Poets writing in English during the last fifty years have freed themselves from a nineteenth-century role which rather comically combined the lay preacher, the parlor philosopher, and the seedy minstrel. Poets in all Western countries, along with artists in general, gradually took upon themselves tasks which required the complete strength of integrated personalities for their accomplishment; and they pushed through experiment and exploration despite the ridicule or the neglect of the public at large. The complexities of the time presented problems whose solution required endurance as well as insight. We are now able to recognize the steps by means of which complicated spiritual and even social situations were laid bare, if not entirely resolved; and the accompanying complicated artistic procedures which often had to be improvised by intuitive means. We can now perceive in what way

. . . the forbidden,
The hidden, the wild outside

was grasped and absorbed into art; and how poets aided not only in the discovery of hidden truths, but had an important part in moulding such discoveries into accessible form.

We are faced, at the end of an era, by two poetic works in English in which the nature of the period's difficulties are made clear—in one of which these difficulties are in some manner transcended. These works are *The Cantos* of Ezra Pound, and T. S. Eliot's *Four Quartets*. *The Cantos* are unfinished; they terminate, at present, with the *Pisan Cantos* (1948), written while Pound was being held prisoner in Italy, at the end of the war, under a charge of treason. *Four Quartets* (1943) consists of four long poems with which Eliot occupied himself in the late thirties and early forties. Both works represent years of technical experiment, as well as of spiritual change, on the part of two highly original but utterly dissimilar men. In each certain central tendencies of the thought of our time are pushed to final conclusions.

Pound never freed himself from an underlying attitude of "enlightened materialism." His beliefs in *The Cantos* have only recently been analyzed with critical detachment. They have been found to be beliefs fixed in the pattern of eighteenth-century Enlightenment; Pound's loyalties are directed toward the Good and Stable State and the Noble Leader. Against his Good (which is always "earth-bound"), Wickedness rather than Evil is arrayed. In a materialist universe, Change becomes the enemy of Permanence; Time is shut away from the Timeless. In the absence of any concept of fundamental Evil, some human conspiracy against the Good Life must be constructed; this conspiracy finally objectified itself in Pound's thought as money, and the manipulation of money known as usury. His passion for the Great Man led him, as Eliot has warned that it must lead anyone, to the worship of Dictatorship. We can see in *The Cantos,* therefore, that as Pound's ideas become more and more obsessive, the logical and unavoidable termination is that system of belief which holds that Man can become God.

It is Pound's tragedy that he clung to this pattern to the point where it cancelled out all earlier preoccupations—even his preoccupation with art. That he advanced into his personal hell without regard for consequences would have lent him a measure of human dignity, if his methods had not deteriorated along with his thinking, to the point of infantile mudthrowing and name-calling. That Pound was forced into the partial humility observable in the *Pisan Cantos* lends that work a certain human pathos. The *Cantos,* from beginning to end—and they are the work of twenty-five years—trace Pound's "die-hard" character. They also trace, however brokenly, his development as an artist. The future must judge whether his crude mistakes in theory and conduct entirely negate his frequent triumphs as a writer.

Eliot passed from his early proud and ironic bitterness, into a long struggle toward centered faith and true humility. The stages of this struggle are plainly evident in his poetry throughout the years. In "Gerontion" not only the personal life but history itself is subjected to a final play of cynical despair. "The Hollow Men" revolves around a point of spiritual stasis: a true "dark night of the soul." *Ash Wednesday* reveals traces of the old irony in full operation, but an irony consciously breaking up before the beginning of faith. *Four Quartets* retraces the steps of a completed spiritual process—the ancient mystical process of gain through loss, light found after darkness, reconciliation reached through dispossession. Here, moreover, Eliot for the first time speaks in his own voice: all masks, all personae, have been relinquished. He turns his face toward the reader, as, with great deliberation, he states what he has experienced on the way through Time to his apprehension of the Timeless. He proffers, as well, a series of purely aesthetic counsels of perfection to the poets of his day. He has gone beyond the point of "explaining the age to itself;" and advanced into those universal regions where the great artist is indistinguishable from the great seer.

v

Eliot has never withdrawn from a constant interest in the possibilities of his medium, or from a continuing desire to reach a larger audience for poetry, by means of poetic drama. He has realized the dangers of modern formalism as poetry becomes more and more synthetic and detached from actual life. The theater has often, in the past, proved itself a revivifying agency for more than one art. Tendencies toward pure abstraction and pure theorizing are checked when the problems of dramatic projection must be faced. Our time has seen modern painting effectively transposed into stage design; and we have heard how the most atonal modern music can gain poignance and power when it interprets dramatic action, as in Alban Berg's *Wozzeck*. Eliot's play, *The Cocktail Party* (1950), was an attempt to re-establish a theater of ideas in contemporary terms; as well as an attempt to discover a level of poetic tone by means of which directness of communication would not be sacrificed to shifts of intensity. It is in this last direction that future poetic experimentation would seem to point: toward a consciously chosen simplicity that can carry meaning, rather than toward any further purification or complication of either material or method.

The later poems of W. H. Auden, particularly the collection *Nones* (1950), point toward another manner of escape from constricting modern formalism. Auden has already explored poetic virtuosity to its limits. In *Nones* he turns away from the dangers of bravura toward a frank and explicit canvassing of "the occasional;" in consequence, he has gained a fresh interest and vigor. He now deals with incidents of everyday life—of friendship and travel, of people and landscape. He is interested in acting, and in being acted upon, in thinking and in feeling. He, too, has a religious faith to which he can relate the operation of emotion and intellect; and the diversified panorama of modern existence he describes is deepened by such relation.

The poet of the future need waste little time and energy in establishing the fact that his art has importance. Neither will he be forced to uncover for himself the scope and difficulty of that art. Eliot speaks of Pound's valuable insistence on "the immensity of the amount of *conscious* labor to be performed by the poet [and on] the kind of training the poet should give himself—study of form, metric and vocabulary in the poetry of divers literatures, and the study of good prose." The results of Pound's "instigations," and of the more intuitive and intellectual findings of Eliot and others now constitute a readily available background and foundation.

In America, a great many of the cultural advantages asked for by Pound in *Patria Mia* (essays on American culture written prior to 1913, but only recently rediscovered and published) have come to pass. Foundations devoted to the subsidy of creative talent generously function. Libraries and museums have opened out and become usable institutions. Certain universities have come to include "creative" courses in their curricula. And, in spite of all evidence to the contrary, as opportunity for the training of talent has broadened, a growing audience has, at the same time, come to appreciate sincere and original work in all fields of the arts.

Some facts remain unaltered. There is always the pedant ready to rigidify creation into codes; Coleridge's fatuous citizen still sits in his eternal cozy armchair. A public, it would seem, must always exist for the sham and the shoddy—one which unceasingly demands stock stimuli, distraction, "entertainment." And it is among this fortunately small, but unfortunately suspicious, public that cries of hatred and ill-will against the artist will originate. Any effort to placate this group is lost; and the poet should waste no time in so doing. Nor should he be startled by either its demands or its resentments.

The poet must continue to recognize both the difficulties and the rewards of his task. In a period of general pessimism, he must not dispense with his inner joy; nor believe in the charts and manifestos of businessmen, philosophers, historians, or warriors. Better by far to listen to the positive voice of Marcel Raymond, an intelligent modern critic, who says: "To maintain that poetry has but little influence in our days is to be blind to the obvious fact that, since romanticism, and particularly from 1912 to 1927, the poet has often performed the function of the lookout aboard ship. It is true that this poetry has few readers, and that it sometimes discourages readers; nevertheless it registers the slightest change in the atmosphere, it makes the gesture that others will imitate and develop (in writings that will be read and rewarded) and it is first to utter the long-awaited word."[2]

2. In *From Baudelaire to Surrealism* ("Documents of Modern Art," Vol. X [New York, Wittenborn Schultz, 1950]).

SELECTED POEMS

LOUISE IMOGEN GUINEY (1861-1920)

In the Reading-Room of the
British Museum

Praised be the moon of books! that doth above
A world of men, the fallen Past behold,
And colour the spaces else too void and cold
To make a very heaven again thereof;
As when the sun is set behind a grove,
And faintly unto nether ether rolled,
All night his whiter image and his mould
Grows beautiful with looking on her love.

Thou, therefore, moon of so divine a ray,
Lend to our steps both fortitude and light!
Feebly along a venerable way
They climb the infinite, or perish quite:
Nothing are days and deeds to such as they,
While in this liberal house thy face is bright.
A Roadside Harp (1893)

STEPHEN CRANE (1871-1900)

Black riders came from the sea.
There was clang and clang of spear and shield,
And clash and clash of hoof and heel,
Wild shouts and the wave of hair
In the rush upon the wind:
Thus the ride of Sin.
Black Riders (1895)

Places among the stars,
Soft gardens near the sun,
Keep your distant beauty;
Shed no beams upon my weak heart.
Since she is here
In a place of blackness,
Not your golden days
Nor your silver nights

Can call me to you.
Since she is here
In a place of blackness,
Here I stay and wait.

Black Riders (1895)

LIZETTE WOODWORTH REESE (1856-1935)

In Time of Grief

Dark, thinned, beside the wall of stone,
The box dripped in the air;
Its odor through my house was blown
Into the chamber there.

Remote and yet distinct the scent,
The sole thing of the kind,
As though one spoke a word half meant
That left a sting behind.

I knew not Grief would go from me,
And naught of it be plain,
Except how keen the box can be
After a fall of rain.

A Quiet Road (1896)

Inscription for a Library

I who am thin with hunger,
I who need bite and sup,
Come to you with my platter,
Run to you with my cup.

A Victorian Village (1929)

TRUMBULL STICKNEY (1874-1904)

Mnemosyne

It's autumn in the country I remember.

How warm a wind blew here about the ways!
And shadows on the hillside lay to slumber
During the long sun-sweetened summer-days.

It's cold abroad the country I remember.

The swallows veering skimmed the golden grain
At midday with a wing aslant and limber;
And yellow cattle browsed upon the plain.

It's empty down the country I remember.

I had a sister lovely in my sight:
Her hair was dark, her eyes were very sombre;
We sang together in the woods at night.

It's lonely in the country I remember.

The babble of our children fills my ears,
And on our hearth I stare the perished ember
To flames that show all starry thro' my tears.

It's dark about the country I remember.

There are the mountains where I lived. The path
Is slushed with cattle-tracks and fallen timber,
The stumps are twisted by the tempests' wrath.

But that I knew these places as my own,
I'd ask how came such wretchedness to cumber
The earth, and I to people it alone.

It rains across the country I remember.
                        The Poems of Trumbull Stickney (1905)

EMILY DICKINSON (1830-1886)

Exclusion

The soul selects her own society,
Then shuts the door;
On her divine majority
Obtrude no more.

Unmoved, she notes the chariot's pausing
At her low gate;
Unmoved, an emperor is kneeling
Upon her mat.

I've known her from an ample nation
Choose one;
Then close the valves of her attention
Like stone.
                Poems by Emily Dickinson (1891)

Hope

Hope is the thing with feathers
That perches in the soul,
And sings the tune without the words,
And never stops at all,

And sweetest in the gale is heard;
And sore must be the storm
That could abash the little bird
That kept so many warm.

I've heard it in the chillest land,
And on the strangest sea;
Yet, never, in extremity,
It asked a crumb of me.
              Poems by Emily Dickinson (1891): 2nd Series

Except the smaller size, no Lives are round,
These hurry to a sphere, and show, and end.
The larger, slower grow, and later hang—
The Summers of Hesperides are long.
                    The Single Hound (1914)

EZRA POUND (1885-   )

Come My Cantilations

Come my cantilations,
Let us dump our hatreds into one bunch
        and be done with them,
Hot sun, clear water, fresh wind,
Let me be free of pavements,
Let me be free of the printers.
Let come beautiful people
Wearing raw silk of good colour,
Let come the graceful speakers,
Let come the ready of wit,
Let come the gay of manner,
        the insolent and the exulting.
We speak of burnished lakes,
And of dry air, as clear as metal.
                    Poems from Blast (1914)

Liu Ch'e

The rustling of the silk is discontinued,
Dust drifts over the court-yard,
There is no sound of foot-fall, and the leaves
Scurry into heaps and lie still,
And she the rejoicer of the heart is beneath them.

A wet leaf that clings to the threshold.

Lustra (1916)

I

E. P. Ode pour L'Election de Son Sepulchre
For three years, out of key with his time,
He strove to resuscitate the dead art
Of poetry; to maintain "the sublime"
In the old sense. Wrong from the start—

No, hardly, but seeing he had been born
In a half savage country, out of date;
Bent resolutely on wringing lilies from the acorn;
Capaneus; trout for factitious bait;

Ιδμεν γαρ τοι πανθ, οσ' ενι Τροιη
Caught in the unstopped ear;
Giving the rocks small lee-way
The chopped seas held him, therefore, that year.

His true Penelope was Flaubert,
He fished by obstinate isles;
Observed the elegance of Circe's hair
Rather than the mottoes on sun-dials.

Unaffected by "the march of events,"
He passed from men's memory in *l'an trentiesme*
De son eage; the case presents
No adjunct to the Muses' diadem.

II

The age demanded an image
Of its accelerated grimace,
Something for the modern stage,
Not, at any rate, an Attic grace;

Not, not certainly, the obscure reveries
Of the inward gaze;
Better mendacities
Than the classics in paraphrase!

The "age demanded" chiefly a mould in plaster,
Made with no loss of time,
A prose kinema, not, not assuredly, alabaster
Or the "sculpture" of rhyme.

from *Hugh Selwyn Mauberly;*
Life and Contacts (1920)

GERTRUDE STEIN (1874-1946)

Water Raining

Water is astonishing and difficult altogether makes a
  meadow and a stroke.

Food: Custard

Custard is this. It has aches, aches when. Not to be. Not to
  be narrowly. This makes a whole little hill.
It is better than a little thing that has mellow real mellow.
  It is better than lakes whole lakes, it is better than
  seeding.

Tender Buttons (1914)

ROBERT FROST (1875-   )

The Pasture

I'm going out to clean the pasture spring;
I'll only stop to rake the leaves away
(And wait to watch the water clear, I may):
I sha'n't be gone long.—You come too.

I'm going out to fetch the little calf
That's standing by the mother. It's so young,
It totters when she licks it with her tongue.
I sha'n't be gone long.—You come too.

After Apple-Picking

My long two-pointed ladder's sticking through a tree
Toward heaven still,

And there's a barrel that I didn't fill
Beside it, and there may be two or three
Apples I didn't pick upon some bough.
But I am done with apple-picking now.
Essence of winter sleep is on the night,
The scent of apples: I am drowsing off.
I cannot rub the strangeness from my sight
I got from looking through a pane of glass
I skimmed this morning from the drinking trough
And held against a world of hoary grass.
It melted, and I let it fall and break.
But I was well
Upon my way to sleep before it fell.
And I could tell
What form my dreaming was about to take.
Magnified apples appear and disappear,
Stem end and blossom end,
And every fleck of russet showing clear.
My instep arch not only keeps the ache,
It keeps the pressure of a ladder-round.
I feel the ladder sway as the boughs bend.
And I keep hearing from the cellar bin
The rumbling sound
Of load on load of apples coming in.
For I have had too much
Of apple-picking. I am overtired
Of the great harvest I myself desired.
There were ten thousand thousand fruit to touch,
Cherish in hand, lift down, and not let fall.
For all
That struck the earth,
No matter if not bruised or spiked with stubble,
Went surely to the cider-apple heap
As of no worth.
One can see what will trouble
This sleep of mine, whatever sleep it is.
Were he not gone,
The woodchuck could say whether it's like his
Long sleep, as I describe its coming on,
Or just some human sleep.

North of Boston (1915)

EDGAR LEE MASTERS (1869-1950)

Petit, The Poet

Seeds in a dry pod, tick, tick, tick,
Tick, tick, tick, like mites in a quarrel—
Faint iambics that the full breeze wakens—
But the pine tree makes a symphony thereof.
Triolets, villanelles, rondels, rondeaus,
Ballades by the score with the same old thought:
The snows and the roses of yesterday are vanished;
And what is love but a rose that fades?
Life all around me here in the village:
Tragedy, comedy, valor and truth,
Courage, constancy, heroism, failure—
All in the loom, and oh what patterns!
Woodlands, meadows, streams and rivers—
Blind to all of it all my life long.
Triolets, villanelles, rondels, rondeaus,
Seeds in a dry pod, tick, tick, tick,
Tick, tick, tick, what little iambics,
While Homer and Whitman roared in the pines?

Spoon River Anthology (1915)

SARA TEASDALE (1884-1933)

When I am dead and over me bright April
   Shakes out her rain-drenched hair,
Tho' you should lean above me broken-hearted,
   I shall not care.

I shall have peace, as leafy trees are peaceful
   When rain bends down the bough,
And I shall be more silent and cold-hearted
   Than you are now.

Rivers to the Sea (1915)

EDWIN ARLINGTON ROBINSON (1869-1935)

Bewick Finzer

Time was when his half million drew
   The breath of six per cent;
But soon the worm of what-was-not

Fed hard on his content;
And something crumbled in his brain
When his half million went.

Time passed, and filled along with his
The place of many more;
Time came, and hardly one of us
Had credence to restore,
From what appeared one day, the man
Whom we had known before.

The broken voice, the withered neck,
The coat worn out with care,
The cleanliness of indigence,
The brilliance of despair,
The fond imponderable dreams
Of affluence,—all were there.

Poor Finzer, with his dreams and schemes,
Fares hard now in the race,
With heart and eye that have a task
When he looks in the face
Of one who might so easily
Have been in Finzer's place.

He comes unfailing for the loan
We give and then forget;
He comes, and probably for years
Will he be coming yet,—
Familiar as an old mistake,
And futile as regret.
            The Man Against the Sky (1916)

New England

Here where the wind is always north-north-east
And children learn to walk on frozen toes,
Wonder begets an envy of all those
Who boil elsewhere with such a lyric yeast
Of love that you will hear them at a feast
Where demons would appeal for some repose,
Still clamoring where the chalice overflows
And crying wildest who have drunk the least.

Passion is here a soilure of the wits,
We're told, and Love a cross for them to bear;

Joy shivers in the corner where she knits
And Conscience always has the rocking-chair,
Cheerful as when she tortured into fits
The first cat that was ever killed by Care.

Dionysius in Doubt (1925)

CARL SANDBURG (1878-   )

Band Concert

Band concert public square Nebraska city. Flowing and
circling dresses, summer-white dresses. Faces, flesh
tints flung like sprays of cherry blossoms. And gigglers, God knows, gigglers, rivaling the pony whin-
nies of the Livery Stable Blues.

Cowboy rags and nigger rags. And boys driving sorrel
horses hurl a cornfield laughter at the girls in
dresses, summer-white dresses. Amid the cornet
stacatto and the tuba oompa, gigglers, God knows,
gigglers daffy with life's razzle dazzle.

Slow good-night melodies and Home Sweet Home. And
the snare drummer bookkeeper in a hardware store
nods hello to the daughter of a railroad conductor—
a giggler, God knows, a giggler—and the summer-
white dresses filter fanwise out of the public square.

The crushed strawberries of the ice cream soda places, the
night wind in cottonwood and willows, the lattice
shadows of doorsteps and porches, these know more
of the story.

Cornhuskers (1918)

T. S. ELIOT (1888-   )

Mélange adultère de tout

En Amerique, professeur;
En Angleterre, journaliste;
C'est à grands pas et en sueur
Que vous suivrez à peine ma piste.
En Yorkshire, conférencier;
A Londres, un peu banquier,

Vous me paierez bien la tête.
C'est à Paris que je me coiffe
Casque noir de jemenfoutiste.
En Allemagne, philosophe
Surexcité par Emporheben
Au grand air de Bergsteigleben;
J'erre toujours de-ci de-là
A divers coups de tra là là
De Damas jusqu'à Omaha.
Je célébrai mon jour de fête
Dans une oasis d'Afrique
Vêtu d'une peau de girafe.

On montrera mon cénotaphe
Aux côtes brûlantes de Mozambique.

Poems (1920)

Marina

Quis hic locus, quae regio, quae mundi plaga?
What seas what shores what grey rocks and what islands
What water lapping the bow
And scent of pine and the woodthrush singing through the
    fog
What images return
O my daughter.

Those who sharpen the tooth of the dog, meaning
Death
Those who glitter with the glory of the humming-bird,
    meaning
Death
Those who sit in the stye of contentment, meaning
Death
Those who suffer the ecstasy of animals, meaning
Death

Are become unsubstantial, reduced by a wind,
A breath of pine, and the woodsong fog
By this grace dissolved in place

What is this face, less clear and clearer
The pulse in the arm, less strong and stronger—
Given or lent? more distant than stars and nearer than the
    eye

Whispers and small laughter between leaves and hurrying
 feet
Under sleep, where all the waters meet.

Bowsprit cracked with ice and paint cracked with heat.
I made this, I have forgotten
And remember.
The rigging weak and the canvas rotten
Between one June and another September.
Made this unknowing, half conscious, unknown, my own.
The garboard strake leaks, the seams need caulking.
This form, this face, this life
Living to live in a world of time beyond me; let me
Resign my life for this life, my speech for that unspoken,
The awakened, lips parted, the hope, the new ships.

What seas what shores what granite islands towards my
 timbers
And woodthrush calling through the fog
My daughter.

Collected Poems (1930)

EDNA ST. VINCENT MILLAY (1892-1951)

Sonnet

Cherish you then the hope I shall forget
At length, my lord, Pieria?—put away
For your so passing sake, this mouth of clay,
These mortal bones against my body set,
For all the puny fever and frail sweat
Of human love,—renounce for these, I say,
The Singing Mountain's memory, and betray
The silent lyre that hangs upon me yet?
Ah, but indeed, some day shall you awake,
Rather, from dreams of me, that at your side
So many nights, a lover and a bride,
But stern in my soul's chastity, have lain,
To walk the world forever for my sake,
And in each chamber find me gone again!

Second April (1921)

Truce for a Moment

Truce for a moment between Earth and Ether
Slackens the mind's allegiance to despair:

Shyly confer earth, water, fire and air
With the fifth essence.

For the duration, if the mind require it,
Trigged is the wheel of Time against the slope;
Infinite Space lies curved within the scope
Of the hand's cradle.

Thus between day and evening in the autumn,
High in the west alone and burning bright,
Venus has hung, the earliest riding-light
In the calm harbour.

Huntsman What Quarry? (1939)

ELINOR WYLIE (1885-1928)

Bronze Trumpets and Sea Water— On Turning Latin into English

Alembics turn to stranger things
Strange things, but never while we live
Shall magic turn this bronze that sings
To singing water in a sieve.

The trumpeters of Caesar's guard
Salute his rigorous bastions
With ordered bruit; the bronze is hard
Though there is silver in the bronze.

Our mutable tongue is like the sea,
Curled wave and shattering thunder-fit;
Dangle in strings of sand shall he
Who smoothes the ripples out of it.

Nets to Catch the Wind (1921)

Felo de Se

My heart's delight, I must for love forget you;
I must put you from my heart, the better to please you;
I must make the power of the spirit set you
Beyond the power of the mind to seize you.

My dearest heart, in this last act of homage,
I must reject you; I must unlearn to love you;
I must make my eyes give up your adorable image
And from the inner chamber of my soul remove you.

Heart of my heart, the heart alone has courage
Thus to relinquish; it is yourself that stills you
In all my pulses, and dissolves the marriage
Of soul and soul, and at the heart's core kills you.
                Angels and Earthly Creatures (1929)

WILLIAM CARLOS WILLIAMS (1883-   )

I

By the road to the contagious hospital
under the surge of the blue
mottled clouds driven from the
northeast—a cold wind. Beyond, the
waste of broad, muddy fields
brown with dried weeds, standing and fallen

patches of standing water
the scattering of tall trees

All along the road the reddish
purplish, forked, upstanding, twiggy
stuff of bushes and small trees
with dead, brown leaves under them
leafless vines—

Lifeless in appearance, sluggish
dazed spring approaches—

They enter the new world naked,
cold, uncertain of all
save that they enter. All about them
the cold, familiar wind—

Now the grass, tomorrow
the stiff curl of wildcarrot leaf

One by one objects are defined—
It quickens: clarity, outline of leaf

But now the stark dignity of
entrance—Still, the profound change
has come upon them: rooted they
grip down and begin to awaken

XXI

so much depends
upon

a red wheel
barrow

glazed with rain
water

beside the white
chickens

Spring and All, I-XXVIII (1923)

H. D. [HILDA DOOLITTLE] (1886-   )

Orchard

I saw the first pear
as it fell—
the honey-seeking, golden-banded,
the yellow swarm
was not more fleet than I,
(spare us from loveliness)
and I fell prostrate
crying:

you have flayed us
with your blossoms,
spare us the beauty
of fruit-trees.

The honey-seeking
paused not,
the air thundered their song,
and I alone was prostrate.

O rough-hewn
god of the orchard,
I bring you an offering—
do you, alone unbeautiful,
son of the god,
spare us from loveliness:

these fallen hazel-nuts,
stripped late of their green sheaths,

grapes, red-purple,
their berries
dripping with wine,
pomegranates already broken,
and shrunken figs
and quinces untouched,
I bring you as offering.
Collected Poems of H. D. (1925)

WALLACE STEVENS (1879-   )

The Emperor of Ice-Cream

Call the roller of big cigars,
The muscular one, and bid him whip
In kitchen cups concupiscent curds.
Let the wenches dawdle in such dress
As they are used to wear, and let the boys
Bring flowers in last month's newspapers.
Let be be finale of seem.
The only emperor is the emperor of ice-cream.

Take from the dresser of deal,
Lacking three glass knobs, that sheet
On which she embroidered fantails once
And spread it so as to cover her face.
If her horny feet protude, they come
To show how cold she is, and dumb.
Let the lamp affix its beam.
The only emperor is the emperor of ice-cream.

To the Roaring Wind

What syllable are you seeking,
Vocalissimus,
In the distances of sleep?
Speak it.
Harmonium (1923)

VACHEL LINDSAY (1879-1931)

The Flower-Fed Buffaloes

The flower-fed buffaloes of the spring
In the days of long ago,
Ranged where the locomotives sing

And the prairie flowers lie low:—
The tossing, blooming, perfumed grass
Is swept away by the wheat,
Wheels and wheels and wheels spin by
In the spring that still is sweet.
But the flower-fed buffaloes of the spring
Left us, long ago.
They gore no more, they bellow no more,
They trundle around the hills no more:—
With the Blackfeet, lying low.
With the Pawnees, lying low,
Lying low.

Going-to-the-Stars (1926)

JOHN CROWE RANSOM (1888-   )

Piazza Piece

—I am a gentleman in a dustcoat trying
To make you hear. Your ears are soft and small
And listen to an old man not at all,
They want the young men's whispering and sighing.
But see the roses on your trellis dying
And hear the spectral singing of the moon;
For I must have my lovely lady soon.
I am a gentleman in a dustcoat trying.

—I am a lady young in beauty waiting
Until my truelove comes, and then we kiss.
But what gray man among the vines is this
Whose words are dry and faint as in a dream?
Back from my trellis, sir, before I scream!
I am a lady young in beauty waiting.

Two Gentlemen in Bonds (1927)

ALLEN TATE (1899-   )

Mr. Pope

When Alexander Pope strolled in the city
Strict was the glint of pearl and gold sedans.
Ladies leaned out, more out of fear than pity;
For Pope's tight back was rather a goat's than man's.

Often one thinks the urn should have more bones
Than skeletons provide for speedy dust;
The urn gets hollow, cobwebs brittle as stones
Weave to the funeral shell a frivolous rust.

And he who dribbled couplets like a snake
Coiled to a lithe precision in the sun,
Is missing. The jar is empty; you may break
It only to find that Mr. Pope is gone.

What requisitions of a verity
Prompted the wit and rage between his teeth
One cannot say: around a crooked tree
A moral climbs whose name should be a wreath.
                    Mr. Pope and Other Poems (1928)

LÉONIE ADAMS (1899-   )

Country Summer

Now the rich cherry, whose sleek wood
And top with silver petals traced,
Like a strict box its gems encased,
Has split from out that cunning lid,
All in an innocent green round,
Those melting rubies which it hid;
With moss ripe-strawberry-encrusted,
So birds get half, and minds lapse merry
To taste that deep-red, lark's-bite berry,
And blackcap bloom is yellow-dusted.

The wren that thieved it in the eaves
A trailer of the rose could catch
To her poor droopy sloven thatch,
And side by side with the wren's brood—
O lovely time of beggar's luck—
Opens the quaint and hairy bud;
And full and golden is the yield
Of cows that never have to house,
But all night nibble under boughs,
Or cool their sides in the moist field.

Into the rooms flow meadow airs,
The warm farm baking smell's blown round,
Inside and out, and sky and ground

Are much the same, the wishing star,
Hesperus, kind and early born,
Is risen only finger-far;
All stars stand close in summer air,
And tremble, and look mild as amber,
When wicks are lighted in the chamber,
You might say, stars were settling there.

Now straightening from the flowery hay,
Down the still light the mowers look,
Or turn, because their dreaming shook,
And they waked half to other days,
When left alone in the yellow stubble
The rusty-coated mare would graze.
Yet thick the lazy dreams are born,
Another thought can come to mind,
But like the shivering of the wind,
Morning and evening in the corn.

High Falcon (1929)

HART CRANE (1899-1932)

The Air Plant

Grand Cayman

This tuft that thrives on saline nothingness,
Inverted octopus with heavenward arms
Thrust parching from a palm-bole hard by the cove—
A bird almost—of almost bird alarms,

Is pulmonary to the wind that jars
Its tentacles, horrific in their lurch.
The lizard's throat, held bloated for a fly,
Balloons but warily from this throbbing perch.

The needles and hack-saws of cactus bleed
A milk of earth when stricken from the stalk;
But this,—defenseless, thornless, sheds no blood,
Almost no shadow—but the air's thin talk.

Angelic Dynamo! Ventriloquist of the Blue!
While beachward creeps the shark-swept Spanish Main
By what conjunctions do the winds appoint
Its apotheosis, at last—the hurricane!

The Hurricane

Lo, Lord, Thou ridest!
Lord, Lord, Thy swifting heart

Naught stayeth, naught now bideth
But's smithereened apart!

Ay! Scripture flee'th stone!
Milk-bright, Thy chisel wind

Rescindeth flesh from bone
To quivering whittlings thinned—

Swept—whistling straw! Battered,
Lord, even boulders now out-leap

Rock sockets, levin-lathered!
Nor, Lord, may worm out-deep

Thy drum's gambade, its plunge abscond!
Lord God, while summits crashing

Whip sea-kelp screaming on blond
Sky-seethe, high heaven dashing—

Thou ridest to the door, Lord!
Thou bidest wall nor floor, Lord!
The Collected Poems of Hart Crane (1933)

MARIANNE MOORE (1887-   )

The Paper Nautilus

For authorities whose hopes
are shaped by mercenaries?
Writers entrapped by
teatime fame and by
commuters' comforts? Not for these
the paper nautilus
constructs her thin glass shell.

Giving her perishable
souvenir of hope, a dull
white outside and smooth-
edged inner surface

glossy as the sea, the watchful
    maker of it guards it
    day and night; she scarcely

eats until the eggs are hatched.
Buried eight-fold in her eight
    arms, for she is in
    a sense a devil-
fish, her glass ramshorn-cradled freight
    is hid but is not crushed.
    As Hercules, bitten

by a crab loyal to the hydra,
was hindered to succeed,
    the intensively
    watched eggs coming from
the shell free it when they are freed,—
    leaving its wasp-nest flaws
    of white on white, and close-

laid Ionic chiton-folds
like the lines in the mane of
    a Parthenon horse,
    round which the arms had
wound themselves as if they knew love
    is the only fortress
    strong enough to trust to.
                        What Are Years (1941)

KARL SHAPIRO (1913-   )

Troop Train

It stops the town we come through. Workers raise
Their oily arms in good salute and grin.
Kids scream as at a circus. Business men
Glance hopefully and go their measured way.
And women standing at their dumbstruck door
More slowly wave and seem to warn us back,
As if a tear blinding the course of war
Might once dissolve our iron in their sweet wish.

Fruit of the world, O clustered on ourselves
We hang as from a cornucopia
In total friendliness, with faces bunched

To spray the street with catcalls and with leers.
A bottle smashes on the moving ties
And eyes fix on a lady smiling pink
Stretch like a rubber-band and snap and sting
The mouth that wants the drink-of-water kiss.

And on through crummy continents and days,
Deliberate, grimy, slightly drunk we crawl,
The good-bad boys of circumstance and chance,
Whose bucket-helmets bang the empty wall
Where twist the murdered bodies of our packs
Next to the guns that only seem themselves.
And distance like a strap adjusted shrinks,
Tightens across the shoulder and holds firm.

Here is a deck of cards; out of this hand
Dealer, deal me my luck, a pair of bulls,
The right to draw to a flush, the one-eyed jack.
Diamonds and hearts are red but spades are black,
And spades are spades and clubs are clovers—black.
But deal me winners, souvenirs of peace.
This stands to reason and arithmetic,
Luck also travels and not all come back.

Trains lead to ships and ships to death or trains,
And trains to death or trucks, and trucks to death,
Or trucks lead to the march, the march to death,
Or that survival which is all our hope;
And death leads back to trucks and trains and ships,
But life leads to the march, O flag! at last
The place of life found after trains and death
—Nightfall of nations brilliant after war.

V-Letter (1944)

ELIZABETH BISHOP (1911-   )

Cirque d'Hiver

Across the floor flits the mechanical toy,
fit for a king of several centuries back.
A little circus horse with real white hair.
His eyes are glassy black.
He bears a little dancer on his back.

She stands upon her toes and turns and turns.
A slanting spray of artificial roses

is stitched across her skirt and tinsel bodice.
Above her head she poses
another spray of artificial roses.

His mane and tail are straight from Chirico.
He has a formal, melancholy soul.
He feels her pink toes dangle toward his back
along the little pole
that pierces both her body and her soul

and goes through his, and reappears below,
under his belly, as a big tin key.
He canters three steps, then he makes a bow,
canters again, bows on one knee,
canters, then clicks and stops, and looks at me.

The dancer, by this time, has turned her back.
He is the more intelligent by far.
Facing each other rather desperately—
his eye is like a star—
we stare and say, 'Well, we have come this far.'
                    North and South (1946)

ROBERT LOWELL (1917-   )

Christmas Eve Under Hooker's Statue

Tonight a blackout. Twenty years ago
I hung my stocking on the tree, and hell's
Serpent entwined the apple in the toe
To sting the child with knowledge. Hooker's heels
Kicking at nothing in the shifting snow,
A cannon and a cairn of cannon balls
Rusting before the blackened Statehouse, know
How the long horn of plenty broke like glass
In Hooker's gauntlets. Once I came from Mass;

Now storm-clouds shelter Christmas, once again
Mars meets his fruitless star with open arms,
His heavy saber flashes with the rime,
The war-god's bronzed and empty forehead forms
Anonymous machinery from raw men;
The cannon on the Common cannot stun
The blundering butcher as he rides on Time—
The barrel clinks with holly. I am cold:
I ask for bread, my father gives me mould;

His stocking is full of stones. Santa in red
Is crowned with wizened berries. Man of war,
Where is the summer's garden? In its bed
The ancient speckled serpent will appear,
And black-eyed susan with her frizzled head.
When Chancellorsville mowed down the volunteer,
"All wars are boyish," Herman Melville said;
But we are old, our fields are running wild.
Till Christ again turn wanderer and child.
                    Lord Weary's Castle (1946)

PETER VIERECK (1916-   )

Of Course Not

The happiest landscape my eyes ever meddled with—
Pines, waterfall, and a most stately lawn—
Is the view they call Paradise Pond in Northampton at
    Smith.
Then comes a hedge, and a hospital farther on.

My boy of three was watching me watch this view
When I heard once more how ambiguous everything is.
He, too, has his dogmas; he "knows" for a fact it is true
That a hurt goes away with a kiss.

My eyes were so full of Paradise Pond I agreed
With my son for an instant as slim as the hedges that
    hide
"Mass. State Hospital" crammed inside
With the crazy and hurt. Is it lack of a kiss
Made the State of Mass. need a house like this?
Of course not. Or, come to think of it, yes indeed.
                    Strike Through the Mask! (1950)

RICHARD WILBUR (1921-   )

In the Elegy Season

Haze, char, and the weather of All Soul's:
A giant absence mopes upon the trees:
Leaves cast in casual potpourris
Whisper their scents from pits and cellar-holes.

Or brewed in gulleys, steeped in wells, they spend
In chilly stream their last aromas, yield
From shallow hells a revenance of field
And orchard air. And now the envious mind

Which could not hold the summer in my head
While bounded by that blazing circumstance
Parades these barrens in a golden trance,
Remembering the wealthy season dead,

And by an autumn inspiration makes
A summer all its own. Green boughs arise
Through all the boundless backward of the eyes,
And the soul bathes in warm conceptual lakes.

Less proud than this, my body leans an ear
Past cold and colder weather after wings'
Soft commotion, the sudden race of springs,
The goddess' tread heard on the downward stair,

Longs for the brush of the freighted air, for smells
Of grass and cordial lilac, for the sight
Of green leaves building into the light
And azure water hoisting out of wells.
                    Ceremony and Other Poems (1950)

W. H. AUDEN (1907-   )

Cattivo Tempo

Sirocco brings the minor devils:
A slamming of doors
At four in the morning
Announces they are back,
Grown insolent and fat
On cheesy literature
And corny dramas,
Nibbar, demon
Of ga-ga and bêtise,
Tubervillus, demon
Of gossip and spite.

Nibbar to the writing-room
Plausibly to whisper
The nearly fine,

The almost true;
Beware of him, poet,
Lest, reading over
Your shoulder, he find
What makes him glad,
The manner arch
The meaning blurred,
The poem bad.

Tubervillus to the dining-room
Intently to listen,
Waiting his cue;
Beware of him, friends,
Lest the talk at his prompting
Take the wrong turning,
The unbated tongue
In mischief blurt
The half-home-truth,
The fun turn ugly,
The jokes hurt.

Do not underrate them; merely
To tear up the poem,
To shut the mouth
Will defeat neither:
To have got you alone
Self-confined to your bedroom
Manufacturing there
From lewdness or self-care
Some whining unmanaged
Imp of your own,
That too is their triumph.

The proper riposte is to bore them;
To scurry the dull pen
Through dull correspondence,
To wag the sharp tongue
In pigeon Italian,
Asking the socialist
Barber to guess
Or the monarchist fishermen to tell
When the wind will change,
Outwitting hell
With human obviousness.

sionist. New York, Charles Scribner's Sons, 1910.

Koch, Vivienne. *William Carlos Williams*. Norfolk, Conn., New Directions, 1950.

Leavis, Frank Raymond. *New Bearings in English Poetry*. New ed. New York, G. W. Stewart, Publisher, 1950.

Lemaitre, Georges. *From Cubism to Surrealism in French Literature*. Rev. ed. Cambridge, Harvard University Press, 1947.

MacNeice, Louis. *Modern Poetry*. Oxford, The University Press, 1938.

Matthiessen, F. O. *The Achievement of T. S. Eliot*. New and rev. ed. Oxford, The University Press, 1947.

Mencken, H. L. *Selected Prejudices*. New York, Alfred A. Knopf, 1927.

————. *A Mencken Chrestomathy*. Edited and annotated by the author. New York, Alfred A. Knopf, 1949.

Monroe, Harriet. *A Poet's Life*. New York, The Macmillan Co., 1938.

O'Connor, William Van. *Sense and Sensibility in Modern Poetry*. Chicago, University Press, 1948.

————. *The Shaping Spirit: A study of Wallace Stevens*. Chicago, Henry Regnery Co., 1950.

Paige, D. D., ed. *The Letters of Ezra Pound*. New York, Harcourt, Brace and Co., 1951.

Pound, Ezra. *Instigations of Ezra Pound,* together with an essay on the Chinese written character, by Ernest Fenollosa. New York, Boni and Liveright, 1920.

Pound, Ezra. *A B C of Reading*. London, Faber and Faber, 1934. Norfolk, Conn., New Directions, 1950.

————. *Make It New*. New Haven, Yale University Press, 1935.

————. *Culture*. Norfolk, Conn., New Directions, 1938.

Ransom, John Crowe. *The World's Body*. New York and London, Charles Scribner's Sons, 1938.

Raymond, Marcel. *From Baudelaire to Surrealism*. New York, Wittenborn, Schultz, Inc., 1949.

Read, Herbert A. *Form in Modern Poetry*. London, Sheed and Ward, 1932.

Richards, I. A. *Principles of Literary Criticism*. New York, Harcourt, Brace and Co., 1925.

————. *Practical Criticism*. New York, Harcourt, Brace and Co., 1929.

Russell, Peter, ed. *An Examination of Ezra Pound*. Norfolk, Conn., New Directions, 1950.

Santayana, George. *Character and Opinion in the United States*. New York, Charles Scribner's Sons, 1920.

Starkie, Enid. *Baudelaire*. New York, W. W. Norton and Co., 1933.

————. *Rimbaud*. New York, W. W. Norton and Co., 1938. Rev. ed. 1947.

Tate, Allen. *On the Limits of Poetry*. New York, The Swallow Press and William Morrow & Company, publishers, 1948.

Unger, Leonard, ed. *T. S. Eliot: A Selected Critique*. New York, Rinehart and Co., 1948.

Williams, William Carlos. *The Autobiography of William Carlos Williams*. New York, Random House, Inc., 1951.

Wilson, Edmund. *Axel's Castle: A Study of the Imaginative Literature of 1870-1930*. New York, Charles Scribner's Sons, 1931.

Wilson, Edmund. *Classics and Commercials: A Literary Chronicle of the Forties*. New York, Farrar, Straus and Co., 1950.

Winters, Yvor. *In Defense of Reason*. New York,

The Swallow Press and William Morrow and C
1947.

Yeats, William Butler. *The Autobiography of W
liam Butler Yeats*. New York, The Macmil
Co., 1938.

————. *Collected Essays*. New York, The M
millan Co., 1924.